8/97

First steps towards an
Acting Career

Nigel Rideout

First steps towards an
Acting Career

Second edition

A & C Black · London

Second edition published 1995
A & C Black (Publishers) Limited
35 Bedford Row, London WC1R 4JH

ISBN 0-7136-4130-4

First published 1991 by Penguin Books

A CIP catalogue record for this book is available
from the British Library.

Cover photograph from a production of
Fiddler on the Roof. Photographer Jerome Yeats,
reproduced with the permission of the
Performing Arts Library (P.A.L.).

Typeset in 9½ on 11½pt Concorde Regular by
Rowland Phototypesetting Limited,
Bury St Edmunds, Suffolk.
Printed and bound in Great Britain by
Biddles Limited, Guildford, Surrey

792.028
RIO
1995

Contents

Appendices

Acting and the Theatre

Dame Judi Dench in conversation with Nigel Rideout

My advice to anyone thinking about a career in the theatre is this: if there is any question in your mind about any other job, then don't act. If, on the other hand, your decision is irrevocable, then you must face up to the knowledge of just how much talent there is about, how many other people have come to the same decision as you and how, the moment you're unable to take on a job, there will be a host of people at your shoulder waiting to take the part over. Also, if you don't have unbounded energy and then some energy to spare, don't even consider acting as a career.

Stamina is vital. An actor's typical day could involve a rehearsal from ten in the morning to six in the evening, followed by a performance that night. Day after day. If after two or three days of this the actor says he's exhausted, then that's an actor who doesn't understand hard work. That's how hard it's going to be. If you can't cope with that schedule, you have no right taking up space in the profession. The audience doesn't pay to come and see you tired or not feeling like it. I'm very lucky in that I can relax and recover very quickly. In fact I can sleep between scenes with no ill-effects – a great advantage.

I set out to be a dancer, then a stage designer and then came to acting on the advice of my brother Jeffrey, who had never wanted to do anything else. He suggested Central School and I was fortunate enough to gain a place, although I'm afraid to say my application was rather half-hearted.

At the end of my first term we were asked to prepare individual mime projects. I had failed to prepare anything and so was forced to do mine straight off the top of my head – I suppose out of a sort of instinct. The teacher, a marvellous actor called Walter Hudd, singled mine out and said, 'Now that's what it's all about!' That gave me great encouragement and suddenly I knew that I was doing the right thing by being there and trying to be an actress.

I'm not sure what the word 'talent' actually means, or what my talent is. I know what I recognise and consider to be talent in others, though my colleagues might not see it or agree with me. Acting is such an impure art. What one person calls great acting another might feel simply doesn't work. As Ralph Richardson said, 'Acting is a puzzling thing. One day it's there and the next nowhere to be seen.'

Your first job after leaving drama school feels like starting all over again. It's a bit like learning to drive a car. It's only after you've passed the test that you actually begin to experience what driving is all about.

I was lucky in that I went straight from Central to the Old Vic Company, where I learned a great many things about acting and about behaviour within a company – something that's vitally important. Unless the members of a company can quickly establish that feeling of being part of one whole, it's very rare for the finished result to be of the highest order. Now that I'm a leading player myself, I find there's the added responsibility of leading by example.

Although there's far more work available in new and varied areas than there was when I was starting out in 1957, sadly the decline of repertory theatre has deprived drama students of that post-training learning and growing experience. Therefore the drama schools have a greater responsibility and need to achieve higher standards within the training period and to tackle a wider variety of subjects.

I think training – and as much training as possible – is essential. It marks the difference between the amateur and the professional. The amateur may be able to play a part three or four times before his voice gives out, but a professional knows how to conserve his energy, breath and voice.

But I do think it's a great failing if the actor thinks he knows it all after three years' training. Always, always, always watch others. Every play I've done in thirty-seven years on the stage has thrown up a new problem, something else I have to learn. The day you think you know it all is the day you should leave the profession.

I feel that the general level of training has risen since my days at Central, especially in specilised areas such as singing. However, I still find all too often at the theatre that I'm seeing television performances. This is a great pity. Maybe students aren't taught enough about projection or are obsessed with realism and method acting, which is fine for their sitting-rooms, but it's no good if the audience can't hear what they're saying or if it muddies the play.

Working on the stage is the thickest part of the wedge; in the middle comes television and the smallest part is film. If you can work in the theatre first, you won't have a big hurdle to jump with regard to the space you're working in. My biggest problem at Central was projection and I remember my teacher, Oliver Reynolds, saying to me, after a long, long pause, 'Well, maybe, Judi, it's because you're a small person and you just can't fill a large theatre.' Well, now I know that I can fill the State Fair Music Hall, Dallas! But I think it was only because of having to face doing it on an American tour. Also, probably, I had been able to gauge my own inadequacies by listening to and watching other people.

Despite success and a lifetime in the theatre, I am always filled with doubts and from time to time have hankerings to do something else within the profession. In the past few years directing plays both professionally and with drama students has given me new stimulus and are experiences I would wish to repeat. Whatever doubts I have, though, I do now know that I'm more use doing what I do than I would be in any other profession: I communicate better as an actress than I would, say, as a social worker.

Read on, and good luck!

Royal National Theatre
1995

Introduction

Many of you will have seen the statistics showing the newcomer's minimal chance of success in the already overcrowded acting profession. If you are easily put off by statistics, by parents, teachers or by hard work, then you are not destined for survival or success as an actor.

For some years there have been far greater opportunities for younger performers in all media and now, sadly, it is the often very experienced and talented middle-aged performers who find it difficult to continue their careers. There are hundreds of people holding Equity cards who no longer act as they have moved on to management, writing or directing. They are not necessarily out of work, although the published figures show them as being so. There are also many Equity members who were given a card for a 'commercial' so that they could advertise their own profession but who have no intention of ever working as professional actors. Lastly, there are those who have cards from who knows where, who constantly turn up, giving awful auditions and clogging up an already overcrowded industry.

The audience finally makes it own choice and will continue to be the arbiter of, one hopes, a general level of good taste. Luckily there are many different audiences to make their own choices. This will keep the business healthy and competitive.

To be fair, everyone should have a chance to prove himself but should not waste the opportunity by being ill-prepared or amateurish in work or outlook. I urge you to use this book and those books recommended in Further Reading to find out as much as possible about the actor's work before you take the first step in any branch of this large and exciting industry.

Acknowledgements

My grateful thanks to the following friends and professional colleagues for their help and contributions to this book: Dame Judi Dench for the Foreword, Prunella Scales, Brigitte Kelly and May Gibb; to all those many people I visited or to whom I wrote and who kindly answered my inquiries; to my mentors from whom I learned so much – Lisle Jones, the late Michael Barry, Michael MacOwan and Joe Mitchenson; and finally, to my unfailingly loyal friend Kitty Black for her carefuly editing and 'Concorde' typing of the manuscript.

N.R.

PART I

Before You Apply to a Drama School

1. A Little History

From Shakespeare's time to the present day, the history of drama training in Britain has involved acquiring practical experience of the fashionable acting style of the day. A few actors, blessed with sure instinct and imagination and a rare and natural insight into dramatic literature, were able to teach themselves the skills required. More usually, however, skills were passed on by experienced actors. Often a performance, including technical business and intonation, would be handed on with a meticulous care for detail. This enables us to know with some degree of certainty the physical and vocal nature of an historic performance – a useful guide before the invention of modern recording equipment. The diaries and journals of actors and critics are also valuable historic references, as are paintings, which can provide a record of attitude, mood, stance and costume design.

Acting style and the standards of performance have varied greatly over the centuries. Contemporary diaries and journals bear witness to how savage the critics were and how abusive an audience could be if they were dissatisfied by what they had paid for. Most present-day actors would be horrified by the violence of the public reaction, but audiences must have been able to maintain a standard of performance, if only by rejecting actors who were incompetent or tedious.

The habit of passing on the details of a particular performance – 'learning by rote', as it is known – persisted in some British drama schools into the 1970s, with venerable retired actors coaching carbon copies of their own performances, often of Shakespearean roles. From a historical perspective this could be fascinating but for a young student it could prove restrictive and highly irritating. The imposition of another actor's performance, which prevents the student from going through his or her own process of exploration and discovery, could by present standards lead to a false and shallow characterisation.

This teaching method is still to be found on the Continent and in Russia. Classical roles in particular are studied in this way. A student will be given an exact intonation for a speech – say, by the seventeenth-century French dramatist Racine – and all the other members of the class will be learning the same speech, with the same phrasing, the same gestures and the same mood. On the other hand, the teaching of contemporary work may be well in advance of British practice.

Formal drama training grew out of the work of the Victorian academies of music and opera and out of private tuition for elocution and deportment. The earliest extant school is the London Academy of Music, where Garcia, a famous Italian mime, gave lessons in operatic gesture at St George's Hall, Langham Place, in 1861. LAMDA (the London Academy of Music and Dramatic Art), as it is known today, added 'Dramatic Art' to its name in the 1920s and has become a major force in the teaching of drama throughout the world.

The Webber-Douglas Academy was also originally an opera school and has moved very successfully into drama as its owners and staff have changed over the years. The same is true of the Royal Academy of Music, which set up a drama department in 1950 in order to help opera singers to act on stage. In time the department outgrew its premises and the establishment was split into two. Rose Bruford left to create her own distinguished college. The other half, under Greta Colson, became the New College of Speech and Drama and is now part of Middlesex University. Other music institutions that have added the teaching of drama to their curriculum include the Royal Scottish Academy of Music, which was founded in 1847, and the Welsh College of Music, which added a drama course as recently as the 1960s.

Although most schools try hard to attract equal numbers of male and female students, women tend to outnumber men by about two to one. This is not the place for an analytical discussion of why this should be, but the reasons may have much to do with the traditional male role of breadwinner and the view of the arts as somehow more suitable for women. In the period after the war it was thought 'sissy' for a boy to want to study ballet, opera or theatre.

Michael Croft, with the establishment of the National Youth Theatre, did much to counteract this attitude. Many of its fine young actors, such as Simon Ward and Michael York, were able to enter the profession without further formal training. Michael Croft also encouraged new writing specifically for young people, including a number of plays by Peter Terson.

Despite the enormous demand for drama training, we still find today that there is a shortage of talented male students. There are far too many establishments for the available numbers of promising students. The larger schools may audition up to two thousand applicants a year, but they maintain that the overall standard is no higher than it was twenty years ago, when the average school auditioned perhaps three hundred a year. It is still as hard as ever to get together a group of twenty-four good students, all of whom can either obtain grants or afford the large fees such intensive training necessitates.

It is interesting to look back over the recent history of drama training in this country to see the path that has finally led to the serious recognition of training, the formation of the Council of Drama Schools and the setting of standards by the National Council of Drama Training (see Appendix II).

The earliest record of a drama school I have found is of one located in Dean Street, Soho, London, in 1834, on the site of the old Royalty Theatre, which has long since been demolished. Miss Fanny Kelly, an actress nearing the end of her career, took number 73 as her private residence. She devoted her savings to 'the realisation of an idea current among lovers of the drama, the creation of a school of acting with a theatre attached'. She obtained the first of a series of licences for daily dramatic readings and twice-weekly theatrical performances. By 1837 she had built a small theatre at the rear of her house, known as 'Duke's Theatre' and 'Royal Dramatic School'. She announced lectures on dramatic acting and engaged teachers for vocal and instrumental music, dancing, fencing and gymnastic exercises. I have found no further mention of the training school, although there is a detailed history of the theatre, which limped on unsuccessfully in the hands of various actress–managers until its closure in 1938.

The Fay Compton Studio was built on the belief that actors were best taught by fellow artists qualified to teach acting, singing and voice, the late Joe Mitchenson, co-founder of the celebrated Mander and Mitchenson Theatre Collection, was a student there in the 1930s:

The studio opened in 1927 in large premises in Red Lion Square, Holborn, under the banner of the highly successful actress, Fay Compton. The course was run and taught by her sister Viola.

Their mother, Virginia Bateman, had run her own studios in the 1890s after she had retired from the stage to bring up her five children. Before she married Edward Compton, who ran the Compton Comedy Company, she had appeared in the Bateman Company at the Lyceum with her sister, Isobel, and a young actor making his London début, Henry Irving.

In such exalted company I found student life pretty daunting – and very hard work. Most of the students were girls, who resented having to take male roles. Alec Guinness was a fellow student with me in the early 1930s and I remember we all found Miss Compton a bit of a dragon, though she was a gifted teacher. Production weeks were the usual saga of rehearsing endlessly until we were all fit to drop. In fact several of the girls did. Up would go the cry from Miss Compton: 'Where's her understudy?'

During my time there the school moved to Soho Square, to rooms above the offices of the *Gramophone* magazine and its recording studios, which were run by Compton Mackenzie, Fay's and Viola's brother. The conflict between serious record producing and student dance classes led regularly to angry notes passing between the floors.

The training was conducted by working actors with a comprehensive outlook on the theatre. Along with all the familiar subjects, there was a heavy emphasis on 'film acting' to cover the vast gap in styles then existing between the stage and the new medium of the screen. Fay Compton herself was present as much as her busy career allowed and she was assisted by Charles Hickman, Clive Morton, Ellen Pollock and Mrs Patrick Campbell's daughter Stella. Viola's motto was that 'An hour with John Gielgud is worth a whole term with the academics.'

The studio's last move was to Baker Street, this time sharing its premises with Eliot Fry, the photographer. It closed at the outbreak of war. The building was blitzed and the studio never opened its doors again.

RADA (the Royal Academy of Dramatic Art) is probably still the most famous theatre school in the world. Soon after its inauguration its first Chairman, Sir George Alexander of the St James's Theatre, wrote the following article in the 1905 *Pelican Christmas Annual*:

So many aspirants are perpetually writing to me asking for advice as to 'how to get on the stage' that I feel a word from me may perhaps be acceptable. If you are in earnest and intend, in spite of all obstacles, to make the stage your profession, 'conjure' your parents or guardians to allow you to enter as a student the Academy of Dramatic Art. There you will be able to go through a settled course of instruction under competent professors; you will, sooner or later, be rehearsed by one of the directors – practical men and women all of them – who are giving their time to this business because they think they are helping an institution which can only be of great service to the young actors and actresses who are to carry on the glorious traditions of the English Theatre. If you show talent you will soon find work at one of the London theatres, or in a provincial company, and you will make your first appearance with some idea of the methods of the profession you propose to adopt. Of course, there are many splendid teachers outside the Academy of Dramatic Art, but this public school of the drama for men and women is a boon to beginners. Surely the young actors and actresses now playing 'thinking' parts in our London theatres find their days of enforced idleness terribly boring. Let them go to the School of Dramatic Art. The stock company is a thing of the past, but if young men who intend to go on the stage will enter the school, they will learn more there in six months than they can hope to learn in any theatre, in these days of long runs, in a year. So take my advice and go to the Academy!

The style may seem antique and amusing to us now but the sentiments still hold good, particularly as there are now so many more outlets for acting skills, all requiring study and experience.

2. Starting Out

The theatre can often have been a career choice made instinctively in early childhood. But is it important to bear in mind that a child who has appeared gifted at acting and singing might, as a young adult, not meet with the same success. A child with a beautiful treble might find that, as he or she matures, his or her voice has little that is exceptional about it. There is no guarantee that a child who has made an impact in *Oliver Twist* or a teenager who has starred in *Gigi* will grow into a successful adult performer. Youthful appeal can quickly evaporate at maturity, leaving little in the way of personality or talent behind.

It is all too easy to be influenced by American 'soaps' such as *The Cosby Show* or *Roseanne*. If you are a serious performer and are faced with opportunities to perform while you are still young, it is vital to be well prepared. Much of what is asked of young performers is not so much acting as 'heightened behaviour'. If that is all you have the knack for, you could find yourself on the scrap-heap before you are out of your teens.

There are good reasons for not embarking on formal acting training too young, before the body is mature enough to accept and respond to advanced techniques and before the emotions have experienced enough to be of use to the imaginative actor. It is true to say that skills are taught but that acting is learned: the acquiring of skill is largely the responsibility of the teacher, but the ability to act must be found within the student him- or herself.

However, there are some performance acts that cannot wait for physical and emotional maturity. Ballet, as a career, has a limited life-span; it is a technical discipline that is best acquired early and pursued steadily. A career in music, too, will benefit from an early start.

What skills can you be acquiring while you are still at school that will stand you in good stead later?

Singing

Singing lessons can be valuable from quite early childhood – although singing in a church choir run by a good choirmaster may teach you just as much and without cost. It is generally accepted that once a voice has broken, formal training should be suspended for about two years. Invaluable skills are the ability to sight-read music and to hold a harmony line. A certain amount of performing experience, either as a solo singer or as a member of a group, will also give good experience of facing an audience.

Dance

Dance classes are an excellent way for the future actor to develop a feeling for style, a sense of space, rhythm, strength and physical co-ordination. Tap is a useful and enjoyable discipline, particularly good for the development of strength and co-ordination. The standard ballroom dances such as the waltz and the quick-step can be easily learned young and may save time and effort later. Examinations both test ability and accustom young dancers to dealing with their nerves.

Music

As well as being enjoyable in itself, learning to play the piano or another musical instrument is a marvellous way to develop concentration, a sense of rhythm and musicality, all of which may be usefully applied to the study of texts at a later date. Playing an instrument also exercises mental and physical co-ordination, sight-reading, memory training and timing.

Speech

With the guidance of a good teacher, speech classes can build confidence and help communication and social skills. It is important that a regional accent or dialect is left alone. A teacher who attempts to force his or her students into producing a colourless 'standard' sound is restricting the development of their as yet only partly formed personalities. It is only actual speech faults that should be ironed out. Although most responsible teachers would see an accent or dialect as an essential part of the individual, they would probably also advocate the ability to use Standard English or Received Pronunciation in order to broaden an actor's potential and enable him or her to satisfy current theatrical taste and to cope more easily with classical texts and the particular speech rhythms called for by such writers as Oscar Wilde, George Bernard Shaw or Noël Coward. It is probably preferable for this aspect of speech training to be left until later.

Sport

The importance of general fitness cannot be overstated. In addition, particular sports bring particular benefits. For example, swimming the breast stroke, if it has been taught properly, encourages the swimmer to breathe in the manner that is required for acting and singing. Specialist sports such as skating, skiing or fencing may well come in useful later.

General Education

Finally, don't underestimate the value of your school work in relation to your chosen career. Foreign languages provide an insight into different ways of expressing oneself and are helpful for accent work. History gives a knowledge and understanding of world events and a sense of how thinking and attitude can change with time and situation. English literature puts into perspective the great ages of drama from the ancient civilisations to the present day. English language offers a familiarity with the construction of your own language, your means of communication, in all its historical and contemporary forms.

In Your Own Time

Try to see as much live theatre as is humanly possible. It doesn't matter whether it is professional or amateur; it will all help you to get to know more about plays and their performance. Watch as much television drama as you can. Persuade your parents to record late-night broadcasts if you have access to a video. Try to watch with a critical and constructive eye. Go to the cinema and/ or hire videos if you can afford it. The more you see the more experience and knowledge you will have and the easier it will be to make decisions about your future.

3. The Next Step

Now you have taken every opportunity to give yourself a broad-based foundation in your school education, you will be thinking about where to continue your full-time training. The first place to consider is probably a drama school.

It is vital that the drama school you choose should offer a validated programme of serious study aiming for the highest standards before graduation. The old regional companies and the touring circuits used to provide young actors with a time to gain experience and hone their skills, but since their decline the drama schools have been required to take their training that stage further so that students are graduating with higher levels of imaginative and technical proficiency. The drama schools have also needed to broaden their curricula to cater for all forms of mainstream live and recorded entertainment as well as being open to fresh and 'alternative' methods and ideas.

Do I need to go to drama school?
Nobody can answer this question for you. It is impossible to make a blanket judgement as factors such as time, age, financial situation, geography and family circumstances will vary so widely.

The case for formal training is a strong one. Exposure to your chosen profession is a great advantage and the more established your school the more of a reputation you will carry with you when you are first starting out in the profession. Once you are on your way the school you trained at will have less and less relevance to casting directors and the theatres employing you. But the most important thing to consider is whether the training is right for *you*.

Now it is no longer possible to work your way through a repertory company over a period of two or three years, starting as assistant stage manager and moving on to acting ASM, before taking small parts and understudying, a drama school is the only place offering that range of experience.

The Pros and Cons of Training

Although personally I would strongly recommend a period of training at a recognised drama school, it is only fair to list some of the arguments against formal training. I set out below the advantages and disadvantages. Many of these points will have already occurred to you, or to your parents or teachers; others may help you clarify what is important to you and allow you to come to the right decision for yourself.

Advantages

- the opportunity to settle in one environment for up to three years to study your chosen subjects without interruption.
- the experience of being part of an ensemble of actors for a prolonged period
- a secure environment in which to grow and mature, developing your abilities and your confidence
- a place to acquire crafts, techniques and specialist skills
- the right, on graduation from a NCDT-approved course (see Appendix II), to be included in *Spotlight* casting directory
- the chance to be seen in performance, during training and at graduation, by casting directors, agents and managements
- the right, on graduation from a NCDT-approved course, to a provisional Equity card if you are offered work within the terms of the Theatre Management Association and Actors' Equity Agreement.

Disadvantages

- the risk of feeling like a fish out of water if your personality is not appropriate to the school
- the risk of feeling restricted by the formal structures of an educational establishment
- you may be happier working on your own rather than in a group
- the specific skills you wish to acquire may be outside the syllabus of the school or dealt with in a more superficial way than you require
- your ideas about performance may be at odds with those of a conventional school
- your natural talent and sense of observation may mean that you are ready to work without giving time to formal training; private tuition to cover particular areas of need may be more appropriate for you

- you may be temperamentally more suited to learning by practical experience – and lucky enough to find a job in which to do so.

What if I don't like it?

Your teachers are likely to say that you are at the school to work hard and learn and that enjoyment is an optional extra. Just because audiences enjoy being entertained, it does not necessarily follow that learning how to entertain should be enjoyable. Acting should be looked on as a craft, a job like any other. It is down to your own effort, commitment and ability to make sacrifices. It is above all important to be honest and not blame others for your own shortcomings.

If you do not enjoy your course, it may be because of the way you are approaching it. That is something only you can change. On the other hand, you may be unlucky and find yourself with an unfortunate mix of students and genuinely find it impossible to learn in such an environment. I have met this situation a few times and where the student concerned has left and rejoined the course at a later date the difficulty has usually been resolved happily.

The old Hollywood legends of actresses plucked from coffee bars and groomed for stardom may thrill the stage-struck public, but the reality of an acting career is somewhat different. Most dedicated actors these days will have undergone formal training. Luck may play a part in your career but if it does come along it will be better served – and is likely to last longer – if it is backed up by thorough training and experience. Finally, a good grounding will help you to cope with success wisely and make better career choices.

4. Being Honest with Yourself

Before you apply to a drama school it is advisable to take a little time to think and ask yourself some searching questions about the choices facing you.

In the acting profession, as in any other profession, standards and levels of commitment can vary wildly. You will meet bad directors, writers, performers and managements. Many talented and sensitive people may lack the ability to survive in such an environment. Some may survive through luck; others will simply disappear. One leading member of the profession who is renowned for her personal warmth and generosity of spirit comments sadly on how difficult it is to continue to be pleasant in such a tough and ruthless profession. Do you have the strength of character to hang on to your own integrity?

Do any of the following comments ring a bell with you from your experience of school plays or amateur dramatics?

'I can't work with that director; he obviously dislikes me and gives me nothing in rehearsal.'
'She thinks she's such a great star she doesn't need any of us.'
'He never even looks at me in our love scene. He must keep his emotions in the fridge.'
'My costume's all wrong for the period and it doesn't fit. Nobody'll listen to me.'
'The play loses its way in the third act. He never rehearses my scenes and spends all his time concentrating on *her* performance.'
'I might as well just not be in the show.'

How easy it is to blame other people for our own shortcomings. All the above moans and groans need to be taken with a pinch of salt. Actors commonly suffer from too much or too little confidence and these are lines that help people get by. Can you keep things in proportion?

We all have ideals and no one would actually advocate putting up with bad standards, charlatans or even, at its extreme, malpractice. But it is important to face up to the reality of an industry that sets out to reflect the conflicts of human existence while producing a few of its own. Idealism without pragmatism is a liability. If you want to stay in the profession, to give of your best whatever the circumstances might be, you will have to learn how to compromise. Can you do that?

Why do you want to act? Don't be deceived by the glossy glamorous image of award nights or chat shows, or by the surge of adrenalin when you see an exciting stage show, film or television play. Feeling the warm response from an audience is a magical experience, but it is no reason to join the profession. Exhibitionism, vanity or self-glorification are the most unhealthy of motivations. What the audience sees is only the tip of the iceberg. What it doesn't see is the hard work, personal sacrifice and emotional endurance. Can you meet those heavy demands?

What sort of actor do you think you are? What sort of actor would you like to become? How do you see your career developing?

- three years at a leading drama school, followed by a provisional Equity card from a theatre-in-education company providing you with a good twelve-month foundation period giving you enough weeks' work to become a full Equity member? (Buy your first Premium Bond.)
- two years in regional theatre with a few voice-overs* thrown in? (Open a savings account for rainy days.)
- one year understudying in the West End with a few small television parts? (Put down a deposit on a flat.)
- a big break into films? (Buy a country cottage.)

There's no harm in setting yourself goals and no virtue in being uncertain or unambitious. But perhaps it's as well to keep your thoughts to yourself – you don't want to appear insufferably over-confident.

Perhaps the most difficult question of all to answer is: what do other people see in you? Talent is an elusive quality that cannot be taught or learned. It seems to exist separately from skill,

---

* Voice-overs, dubbing or post-synchronisation, adding voices to film for original soundtrack commentary, substituting for a pre-recorded voice or providing English-language dialogue for foreign films, can be a lucrative business if you have a gift for accents and dialects. Many actors can fit in the odd session in their lunch hours or between rehearsals.

technique and knowledge. People instinctively spot it in others and it is possible to know instinctively yourself that you possess that 'special something'. It is almost indefinable, but seems to be made up of a combination of the following:

- the ability to translate life experiences
- an open and generous spirit fired by an exciting energy
- a strong eye focus filled with thought and commanding attention
- great warmth
- a sense of danger
- courage
- sensitivity and vulnerability

It is asking a lot to find all these qualities in one person and, indeed, many successful performers appear to possess very few of them. Nevertheless, even glimpses of some of them will set you apart and with the acquisition of technical skill and a knowledge of your own potential they can be more fully revealed. Seek the advice of other people – preferably not close friends who might say only what they think you want to hear – although they may say that it is too early to see how you might develop. But remember, if you do seek serious advice, you must be prepared to face the truth.

5. Researching Your Training

Any academy is only as good as its current staff and students. The fact that Laurence Olivier trained there sixty years ago may be a matter of interest, but it will be no help to you in deciding where to apply now. It is important for you to find the right environment in which you can study and develop. What may suit your best friend may not be right for you. Thorough research now will pay dividends later. The wrong atmosphere could badly restrict your potential growth or destroy your confidence. Remember the maxim: 'It can take years to build confidence and only seconds to destroy it.' Staff and students can have the most positive and also the most devastating effect on each other.

Another initial word of warning. Some schools need you more for your fees than for your talent. Some need to keep up their numbers in order for the course to be recognised for local-authority support or government funding. This is known in the business as 'carrying dead wood'. Dead wood is the last thing you want to be. One of the more despicable practices of unscrupulous schools is carrying students for a year and then dropping them.

One good way to gauge the general feeling of a school is to see one of its public productions. If it means a trip to London and you can stay a few days – perhaps you have a kind relative? – if you time your visit right you might even catch several productions from different schools.

Try to have a good snoop round while you are there, sensing the atmosphere of the place. If possible, talk to current students and try to find out what they think about their course. Use your instincts – after all, so much of an actor's life is geared to instinct, this is a good opportunity to make use of it.

If your school is arranging a trip to, say, a London museum, it might be possible for you to organise a visit to a drama school and a meeting with a member of staff there. Or perhaps your school careers officer might invite someone from a drama school to come and give a question and answer session at your school. This might be most economically arranged by bringing together interested pupils from a number of local schools.

These things won't be arranged unless you push for them. So make a bit of a nuisance of yourself and don't give up – although it is advisable to use a little cunning to make sure you appear to be motivated by an irrepressible enthusiam for life and learning. What better way to try out your acting abilities in a real-life situation!

With as much research under your belt as you can afford, absorb and digest, the time has come to send for the prospectuses of the schools that interest you. Read carefully the philosophy of the training, study the facilities and be objective. Are they telling you everything you want to know? If not, phone the school switchboard and ask the receptionist to fill in the gaps.

For instance, the sizes and make-up of the student groups are not always given. Do you want to be in an acting class of twenty-four, of whom twenty are women? Imagine Viola shared between six women, or Hamlet between eight men. Unless such a group is usually divided for most of the sessions, this is an impossible way to work. In a two-hour acting class of twenty students, everyone can work together, which will be useful for many exercises, but if the class is geared to solo work, no individual student will have the attention of the teacher for more than about six minutes. This problem can be particularly acute with money-making summer schools or community weekend courses and can cause the serious student great disappointment.

Generally a group of eight to twelve is ideal if the class duration is sufficient to allow for both personal individual attention and for the camaraderie of group experience, so necessary for an actor who wishes eventually to become a member of a company.

If the idea of group work does not appeal to you, it is as well to recognise it early on. There are some people, however, who find themselves cramped by group and school disciplines, and if you are one of these perhaps you should reconsider whether a drama school is the best place for you. It is also possible that a solo performer might do well to learn initially from a group and then follow his or her personal route at a later date. But there are no rules – trust your instinct.

Validation

The Conference of Drama Schools (CDS) consists of eighteen academies or colleges who run courses approved by the National

Council for Drama Training (NCDT). (There are a few schools outside the CDS which have NCDT-approved courses.) NCDT approval means that over a period of days a group of professional 'experts' has inspected the premises, sat in on classes and talked to members of staff and students in order to set a level below which training should not fall. This system has been in operation since 1976 and provides guidance for funding and grant-giving bodies.

The NCDT has also been instrumental in devising an agreement between Equity and the Theatrical Management Association (TMA) whereby new graduates from NCDT-approved courses can join a register which will guarantee them a provisional Equity card if they are offered a job within two years of completing their training. The TMA reserves the right to cast actors not from NCDT-approved courses and the agreement allows one Equity card per year for each subsidised management for a newcomer from any source. Commercial producers in the provinces also have the right to take on newcomers. They have secured a pool of 250 cards to be divided equally between NCDT-approved graduates and those from elsewhere.

What are the implications of this agreement for your time at drama school? It would be sad if the prize of a greater chance of a provisional Equity card meant that you were prepared to put up with less than satisfactory conditions in order to graduate from a NCDT-approved school.

If that sounds contradictory, let me explain. At the time of their inspection the visiting professionals will see everyone on their best behaviour with teachers working to make class content as good as it can possibly be. What the inspectors won't see is the teacher who can teach an excellent class when required to do so but who can be lazy and ill-prepared for the rest of the year. Students who fear that to complain about any aspect of their course will result in their being cast badly will not feel able to discuss their reservations openly with the inspectors.

The lack of adequate student representation is a worrying element in some schools. The cost of training and supporting oneself over a period of three years is a major investment and students are anxious not to jeopardise their opportunities. It is essential to have an atmosphere in which difficulties between staff and students can be aired safely and tensions are not allowed to run riot, damaging the student's progress and confidence.

Above all, it is very difficult for the inspectors to make a thorough examination of the syllabus. Teachers and principals will talk happily about the subjects on offer but getting them to discuss the what, how and why of the courses is quite another matter.

The acting course itself is often the most difficult to pin down. I was interested to find as I was researching this book that many people responsible for organising acting courses would go to any lengths to avoid explaining the nuts and bolts of their teaching methods, usually limply quoting some such phrase as 'You can't teach people to act; they can only learn by experience.'

There are of course exceptions. Some schools, for example the Drama Centre, advertise a strict methodological approach and philosophy so that the student will know precisely what he or she can expect from the course and whether it is what he or she would want if selected by the school. Here is the Drama Centre's admirable declaration of its philosophy:

> The training is systematic. It develops from class to class, from term to term. It is this methodological bias that distinguishes it from other schools, most of which adopt a pragmatic approach to the problems of training. In the pragmatic school acting is taught largely by example, through working with professional directors on a variety of plays and learning how to meet their requirements. The methodological approach is different. Within it the Acting Class is of central importance. This class is based on the assumption that there are certain general problems which can be abstracted for purposes of study from the specific problems of any given piece and 'technique' defined by a mastery of these problems rather that by mechanical finesse.
>
> The approach in this school derives from a fusion of several major contributions to the development of European theatre in the twentieth century. These include:
>
> *The Stanislavsky Method*
> The most famous and detailed of all methods and the point of departure for most subsequent developments; those of Grotowski as much as those of Brecht. The school belongs within the central tradition of Occidental realism.
>
> *The Achievement of Rudolf Laban*
> The architect of the European Modern Dance, one of the few great visionary innovators whose scrutiny was directed towards the phenomena of the expressive power of movement in all its manifestations. It is his ideas which in particular influenced the work of Michael Chekov, a forefather of 'The Method' in the United States. The international standing of the Drama Centre derives very particularly from this work as developed by Yat Malmgren.

6. The Application Form

The questions set out below will give you some idea of what to expect from a drama school application form. It might be useful for you to spend a little time considering these questions and devising clear, concise answers. A well-presented, tidy form giving evidence of clear thinking will create a good impression. If your handwriting is erratic or difficult to read, it might be advisable to type your answers.

First you will be asked some straightforward factual questions:

Age
Height
Weight
Hair colour
Eye colour
Secondary school
Examinations passed
Further education
Special training (singing, ballet, musical instrument, acting, technical, etc.)
Professional/amateur theatre experience
Other employment

Then you will be asked some more searching questions about yourself:

What has led you to believe you want to be a professional actor?
Give a brief statement of your ambitions in terms of a career in the professional theatre or in other media.
State briefly any further details of experience or personal details you feel may be relevant. Why are you applying to this school in particular?
Have you written anything or organised any events?

Are you good with people and do you observe life?

How much experience do you have outside school, home, club? For instance, have you travelled, undertaken full- or part-time work, taken part in sporting activities, etc.?

Do you know what you want out of life?

How often have you been to the theatre in the last twelve months?

You will also be asked to provide a photograph of yourself. Choose a sensible full-face shot.

7. Audition Procedure

You will arrive at a reception area where your name will be checked and ticked off a list. Make sure you see someone as soon as you arrive. It is possible that you may be offered the opportunity to audition immediately if other people have cancelled or been delayed. Avoid the temptation to be heroic – you might need to recover from a long and awkward journey or you might be wet through or mentally disorganised. This is *your* choice and you will have paid a fee for the audition, so refuse to be rushed and ask for a reasonable time to prepare yourself.

You are likely to find yourself with other applicants. Everyone will be nervous, so be sensitive to the feelings of your companions and don't be intrusively chatty or falsely cheerful. You will all need to be quiet in order to keep up your concentration and prepare yourselves without distractions. There should be a room available for you to change in, do some vocal exercises and/or a physical warm-up and perhaps run through your audition pieces.

Once inside the auditorium or audition room, you may be invited to sit and chat for a few minutes with the audition panel. Some schools offer you the choice of which you would prefer first, the interview or the speeches. Be prepared and make a positive decision. 'I don't mind' is no help to the panel and is likely to make you feel even more uncertain of yourself.

The conversation will take your application form as its starting point. Have something to say about your work so far and your hopes for the future. You might be asked about the last play you saw. Other questions might include why you are auditioning for this particular school, and if you are auditioning elsewhere and were offered several places, which you would take up. Do think carefully about your answers. If you plan to play politics, you had better be good at it! Don't brag: 'My mother knows so-and-so'; 'My father is . . .'; 'I met so-and-so'. No one will be impressed. It's what you can do that's important, not who you know. Above all, don't gush.

You are likely to be asked if you have already played the parts you have taken your audition speeches from, whether you have seen them performed and whether you have had any help with the preparation of your performance. These are important questions. The idea behind an audition is to see how *you* work and what ideas and imagination *you* bring to bear on a text. The last thing the panel wants to see is an impersonation of the interpretation of a private coach.

A famous Broadway actress of the past used to coach at a New York academy. Whenever one of her female students auditioned they invariably offered Blanche Dubois from *A Streetcar Named Desire*. Year after year I watched them sitting in the identical position with the identical props and interpretation, giving uninspired faded carbon copies of a once great original.

Most professional directors say that they know almost as soon as an actor walks through the door whether they are suitable for a part. Others say that they have made up their minds after the first thirty seconds of an audition speech. The remainder of your speech gives them a chance to look at your physical qualities in more detail. The tougher directors sing out 'Thank you!' almost before an actor has breathed in.

The drama school audition is rather different, although no less frightening. At least the panel knows that you want to be trained and isn't expecting you to be perfect. The panel will usually try to help you to do your best. Do not try their patience by ignoring the required duration of the speeches. The average limit is three minutes, though personally I believe two minutes is more than enough. Even if you are good, the chances are that the longer you carry on, the less good you will be.

Panels will usually tell you to 'begin when you're ready' – so *be ready*. It is infuriating when a student walks on stage and announces that he or she needs a couple of minutes to get into the part. If everyone behaved like that, the audition day would never end. Between your speeches the panel might want you to wait while they make notes. If they do not ask you to pause beforehand, do ask if that is what they want. However, if they leave the choice to you, you may find it preferable to move almost straight on to your second speech, using the impetus of the first piece to drive you on, particularly if you have devised a neat way of changing from one character to the next.

The most impressive audition I have ever taken was by an

English actor who is now very successful. He walked confidently on stage, announced his first piece and performed with gusto, attack and energy. When he had finished he walked upstage in a half-circle as he put on a corduroy cap he had taken out of an inside pocket and then turned downstage as a completely new character. It was a remarkable transformation – talented, skilled and elegant. As he finished the second piece, he whipped off the cap, half bowed to us, said thank you and left the stage. By that time we were tempted to rush after him and drag him back for more – in fact, we were reacting just like an ideal audience.

That moment was so remarkable because of the actor's professionalism. Naturally it is a rare occurrence at drama school auditions. If it were not, the schools would have no worthwhile role.

One advantage of a short text is that the panel might take time to rework the speech with you. They might ask you to present the speech in a different way, not because what you offered them was necessarily wrong, but because they want to see how adaptable you are and how quickly and willingly you take direction. Do not be surprised if they ask you to sit down at a non-existent coffee table in a canteen and imagine you are talking to your worst enemy using your Hamlet soliloquy. Their instructions might appear bizarre but go for the exercise with courage. Forget all your careful preparation and you may be surprised how the thoughts are rekindled in your mind and the argument of the speech strengthened by a new focus and situation. Rarely will the panel's requests be mere gimmicks; they will be tried and tested ways to redirect your work in a way that reveals more of you as an actor. They will admire your pluck for having a go. Whatever you do, don't try to talk your way out of the exercise by finding some brilliant argument to show the request is not valid or meaningful.

During your visit to the school, you may be required to take part in a number of solo or group sessions so that your various abilities and skills can be assessed.

Improvisation

You might be asked to perform a solo exercise by a member of the panel. Do not be surprised or upset if you are asked to do something different from other people – or not asked at all. The panel may already have seen from your piece what it was they needed to know about you.

In a typical group improvisation, you might be asked to lie on the floor as if you were in bed at home alone. When the instructor claps his or her hands you wake up slowly and find yourself in a box with the rest of the group, whom you have never seen before. The only restriction on the exercise is that there is no way out of the box.

The improvisation can be taken in any way you like. Nothing has been said about the size, shape, atmosphere or structure of the box; that is for the group to work out. What the panel or instructor needs to see is how far your imagination can stretch, how readily you react to each other's ideas and how easily you can break out of the bonds of naturalism. The key is to be brave. Nothing can be achieved if your imagination remains strictly literal. It is also important for the school to see how you work in a group. Are you helpful? Do you opt out? Do you try to take over? How freely do you adapt and incorporate other students' ideas? Does your imagination remain pedestrian and predictable?

Two-handed exercises give a more personal insight into your imagination. You must be ready for anything, but don't feel obliged to be funny or to 'succeed'. Try to be energetic, receptive and imaginative and try not to feel threatened.

You might be asked to go up on stage two at a time to develop a scene from a line given to you by the instructor. As soon as the line is given it must be spoken by the student as if it were the opening of a scene. If it is instantaneous there is no time to decide who you are, where you are or what you are doing. The scene continues until the instructor calls a halt.

The object is to see how well you can keep going and respond to any situation thrown at you. An example might be 'For goodness' sake, put your trousers on!' A response of 'No' or 'Why?' is very unhelpful to a partner and leaves him or her to invent the circumstances of the scene unsupported.

Singing

The importance placed on hearing you sing will vary from school to school. If you can sing, prepare a couple of songs in your range and bear in mind you will be singing from a stage, not with a microphone. Accompany yourself on a guitar if you are able to, or bring a portable *battery*-operated cassette player. Don't choose a song that usually has a complicated orchestration if you are going to be singing unaccompanied. A simple country or folk tune will show the naturally expressive quality of your voice to good effect. You might be asked to do some sight-reading and you might be

given an ear-test to discover whether you are pitch- or tone-deaf.
If you are at all unsure of the quality of your singing, the answer is
don't.

Movement

An instructor may take a group session, leading you through
simple sequences of steps to piano or drum accompaniment. This
will reveal if you suffer from two left feet, flat feet, a sway back, are
grossly overweight or lack a sense of rhythm or basic physical co-
ordination. It will also show the degree of development of your
physical expression and body language.

If you are not offered a place at the school there might be a
number of reasons for your failure. It might reflect on a poor
choice of audition piece or on your basic acting ability. The panel
might like your work despite a poor audition and be interested
enough to rework the piece for you. This may be a great help for
any future auditions, so be prepared to accept their help.
    Other reasons for failure may be

- that you have no obvious talent or you do have talent but
  not of the sort the school can help.
- that you are talented but have too many physical or vocal
  problems to be ironed out in the available time. A school
  cannot cater for students with flat feet, nodules, deviated
  septums, sway backs or insufficient command of the
  English language.
- that you are too young for the type of training the school
  offers. This may not be simply your chronological age, but
  you may as yet be too immature and lacking in life experience. On the other hand, you could be too old and set in
  your ways and unable to mix with a younger group.
- too many students of your type may already have been
  offered places. The school will want to balance the year
  group in order to give all students an equal chance of good
  casting.

It is not really possible for a school to give everyone full reasons
why they have not been accepted. Some schools may suggest that
you apply again the following year if it is felt that you would
benefit from the delay. It would be highly unsatisfactory for you to
be in a group where there were half a dozen other students all with
identical physique, colouring and attitude. These are hard truths

to face but you must develop the fibre and mental stamina to take this kind of knock if you are to survive in this competitive business.

Some schools offer waiting-list places. This can be more positive than it might at first appear as many students will be unable to take up their places for one reason or another. If you are offered a waiting-list place, try to keep your options open as late as possible: you could be called within a week of the start of term.

8. Choosing Your Audition Speech

Schools set out their audition requirements in their prospectuses and these may change from year to year. Some give you a list of texts to choose from and this certainly relieves you of the worry of finding a suitable piece for yourself.

My own preference is for a free choice, as none of the suggested pieces may suit you or show you to best advantage. A free choice also allows the student to use a less well-known classical piece or to string together intelligently a series of short speeches to make up the required length. The panel is likely to know the piece that you choose, but your performance should explain the circumstances of the speech to anyone who does not know it. Avoid the need for lengthy, time-wasting introductions.

The Classical or Shakespeare Speech

It is wise to ask yourself why you are required to perform a classical speech. What does the panel want?

- to hear how you use words not in your everyday vocabulary
- to hear how you use words that carry a greater descriptive content than contemporary speech
- to see how you handle yourself physically in a larger-than-life situation
- to see how you use your imagination to deal with matters outside your own experience.

You may be restricted to Shakespeare or you may be able to choose from any play written between 1550 and 1800. If the latter is the case you have an enormous range available to you. Most important, perhaps, is to bear in mind a good balance and contrast with the contemporary piece.

It might pay to be original. Many an audition panel groans inwardly when for twenty-five years, several hundred times a year, they've been faced with Little Henry announcing he is going to give his Bottom from *A Midsummer Night's Dream* and with Big Jane offering her Viola from *Twelfth Night*, particularly if neither realises they are involved in a comedy. It would not be surprising if the panel's judgement were to be clouded by natural prejudice.

The Contemporary Speech

Again, you may be restricted to a given selection of speeches. If not, there is no need to be shy about writing a piece for yourself if you think you have the skill and feel it will work for you. Novels and film scripts as well as plays may yield a marvellous passage for you.

What are you showing the panel this time?

- a good contrast with the classical speech, for example in weight, style or humour
- where you are now as an actor in the 1990s
- that you can communicate directly and honestly in your own language and accent or dialect.

In choosing your texts, look for pieces with a strong focus and clear thought patterns. Ideally the speeches should make complete sense without any need for introduction or explanation. See if the text has a distinct beginning, middle and end and that its structure will work away from the context of the play. If the circumstances are not defined or the argument is not strong enough, it is legitimate for the purposes of an audition to take the text away from the context of the play and reinterpret it. Remember that the panel will be more likely to concentrate on your work if you choose a piece that expresses one big thought clearly rather than one that is a long meandering aimless passage.

Do not worry too much about not being the appropriate age for the role, particularly for the classical/Shakespeare piece. The panel understands that you are only eighteen or whatever, and that all through your training you will be taking on roles well outside your own age range, both as a casting convenience and as an exercise to stretch your technique and imagination. While perhaps avoiding the obviously aged characters, such as Lear or John of Gaunt in *Richard II*, make your choice from as wide a range as possible. Performance is less to do with age than with weight, build, wisdom and humour.

Avoid a speech from a part you have already played in a school or amateur production unless you are absolutely confident that it can be made to work without all the trappings of lighting, scenery and costume, and without the other actors. You will find it hard to forget the details of the production. Without the gold-painted staircase behind you or the forty peasants cheering you on or that wonderful costume, the moment may not be quite so magical. The panel will see only what you show them and not the marvellous memories you are carrying in your mind.

A list of suitable audition speeches is given in Appendix I.

9. Preparing Your Audition Speech

You will be offered all sorts of advice on the best way to cope with your nerves and create the relaxation needed for your audition. Here are a few practical suggestions to help you make the most of this first opportunity in your career. In all aspects of your preparation, *simplicity* is the keyword.

Choose your two speeches, but also have a standby in case one of them proves unsuitable. Don't be afraid to change. The important thing is for you to be as comfortable as possible. It is even possible that a panel might ask you if you have prepared a third piece.

Type or write out your pieces with great care, making sure that you are copying the text and the punctuation accurately. Leave a space between each line so that you can add interpretation or staging notes. Have a second clean copy with you at the audition in case the panel would like to see it if it is unfamiliar to them or they want to follow the text or prompt. Plastic see-through folders are good for this purpose, as they are both practical and smart.

Study the pieces by listening to yourself speaking them out loud, so that you learn the text by its *sound*. So much of the dramatic action is in the sound and shape of the words. This is particularly true of Shakespeare's texts.

Set out with the idea that you need nothing but the text. You don't need anything or anyone else to make sense of the speech. Should you reach a point in rehearsal when you simply can't achieve your performance without reference to another character or to a prop or piece of furniture, then that is the point at which you can allow them to be introduced. Try above all to keep your interpretation as straightforward and as uncomplicated as you can.

Staging

Do not plan to include the panel as part of the scene. Their job is to be an expert audience watching you. Even if the script requires you to address the audience, if you speak directly to the panel they will be unable to concentrate on your work. You might even embarrass them into looking down at their papers in order to avoid eye contact with you.

An actor can command an area in front of him or her in an arc of about 120 degrees. You will naturally imagine the panel sitting square on to you in the middle of this area. If you need to place another character on stage with you, set him within this angle. Do not address other characters as if they are offstage, either prompt side (on your left as you face the audience) or stage right (opposite prompt), as this will mean you are standing in profile to the panel and your playing will become rather two-dimensional and consequently lack expression. Avoid facing upstage (with your back to the panel) except for a momentary effect.

Do not count on a panel member reading in another character's lines for you. It is distracting for them to have to cue you and will stop them concentrating on your performance.

Do not plan your staging to be too rigid. You may well have to be adaptable. The audition might take place in a small room or a cavernous auditorium. In any event the location will be nothing like the bedroom you have so carefully rehearsed in. If you are thrown by anything, try not to let it show and make adjustments quickly and without fuss. It is a sign of a true professional.

Stage Management

You have immense choice when it comes to your physical performance. You can kneel, sit on your haunches, lie on the floor, stand, lean against a pillar or a wall or a proscenium arch. With all this choice it should be possible to do without tables and chairs so that the maximum time can be spent on your performance and not on your stage management.

Be professional from the outset. If you keep it simple and streamlined you will be your own best stage manager. It is not unknown for a nervous student to waste valuable minutes positioning a chair only to ignore it throughout his or her performance. Limit your props. It is permissible, for instance, to tear up a letter if it is an integral part of a scene, but remember that the panel may not take kindly to having to clear up your cigarette ends, scraps of paper, smashed glass or spilled water.

If you plan to use items of costume, do not wait until you are called before getting them ready. Then is not the moment to put on those boots with the very complicated laces. Plan to avoid an awkward pause between your speeches by reducing any costume to the simplest possible. For instance, you might take off a practice skirt used for your Shakespeare speech to reveal trousers for your contemporary piece. You could then remove the trousers to reveal footless tights and leotard for any movement or improvisation class. Women can pin up their hair for one speech and then let it fall loose for the second, giving an effective contrast in line and style. There is nothing to stop you wearing a hairpiece or a wig as long as it can be easily removed.

Choose clothes appropriate for the period and style of the speech. This sounds obvious but there has been many a Masha who has struggled to make *The Three Sisters* convincing in slacks and high heels. A clear line in costume leads to clear and direct physical expression to support the thoughts and words. You may want to wear your favourite clothes or deliberately 'dress down', but put the needs of your audition piece first. If your hair has a tendency to fall over your forehead and eyes, keep it back with a headband or sweatband to keep your face free and open.

Structuring Your Speech

Because your chosen text has been taken out of the context of the play, you will need to invent a clear, strong opening, perhaps with a focused movement or sound to attract attention and let the panel know in no uncertain terms that you are up there working and want to be watched. (Do not be put off if you catch them writing notes out of the corner of your eye.)

You might decide to start your piece by facing upstage, taking a breath and using the energy of the breath to turn swiftly around to face the audience projecting your eye focus directly above the panel or to one side of them. The speech might start actually on the turn, strengthened by the effect of the movement, or you might prefer to suspend the words by several beats, as long as you can maintain the energy you have just generated to fuel the speech when you do start.

If you breathe out after the turn and physically collapse in any way, you will need to breathe in again in order to speak and get the energy back. Doing that will lose all dramatic impetus and you will also have lost the purpose of the move. Of course, there will always be a circumstance that will require whatever it is you are being advised to avoid. It will be right because there is a context to support it. To pursue our example, you might start a speech by turning angrily to face someone, then control yourself, breathe out, relax inside and begin to speak in a calmer vein as the character decides to change the subject or the nature of the relationship.

You might want to start by running in from offstage and throwing yourself on the floor in hysterical laughter. Whatever suits the piece out of the context of the play is fine – as long as it is positive, bold and relevant.

Panel members are often unsure whether a performance has started or, indeed, ended. Some students seem to want to start a scene with the character thinking to him- or herself for several minutes. You must not be surprised if you try this to find the panel assumes you have forgotten your lines.

If you are asked to go straight on to the second speech, be swift in executing any change you have organised. Whip off your practice skirt while moving into the next scene or let your hair down as the new character emerges into the new environment you have created in your imagination. Practise these mechanical changes over and over again until you are confident that even with a bad attack of nerves nothing can go wrong.

Make the end of your speech as definite as the beginning. If possible, turn upstage and cut yourself off by breathing out and relaxing. Turn round and say thank you to the panel. It is not advisable to spend two minutes crumpled up against a wall convulsed in tears to show how anguished you have become while leaving the panel completely unmoved. You will only embarrass and irritate them if they think you have had the most wonderful indulgent time while they have been profoundly bored.

Learning Lines

Learning lines is rarely easy. However, you will make the job far harder for yourself if you try to learn the lines before you learn the sense. Acting books often advise you to mark up the text into sense beats – units of a single idea. Once you have established the structure of the speech, you will find it much easier to commit to memory, as you will understand exactly why and how ideas develop and follow one on the other.

When you think you know the lines thoroughly, do a speed run with a friend. Say the text as fast as you possibly can while your friend marks the passages that cause you trouble. Go over the weak lines at least a dozen times each, again very fast in order to build up a strong photographic and motor memory of the particular fragment. Now try the speech again and see if you have improved.

Once you have eradicated the weak spots, make it harder for yourself. Try speaking the text while mowing the lawn or washing up or cleaning the car. The distraction of physical activity will force you to concentrate all the harder. If you find you have to stop the activity in order to remember the lines, they are not secure enough yet.

The final test is to say the speech while battling against loud music, preferably something like Wagner's *Ring*, which is very dramatic, irregular and noisy. If you can survive that, then you really are home and dry. Modern disco-style music does not have the same effect. You will be lulled by the regular beat and will find that you can simply ignore it.

If you do forget your lines during your audition, do not swear, look at the panel in fright and burst into tears. They are very understanding and are quite used to nerves causing all sorts of problems. Nor do you need to ask permission to start again or pick up where you left off. Simply stop, breathe, gather your composure and go quietly on. It may be that they do not even notice that you lost your way. Never shout for a prompt. This is a terribly amateur habit. Many drama schools do not allow prompting at all during performances so that students learn not to rely on a safety net right at the outset of their careers.

Let us take a couple of examples to see how you might set about preparing your audition speeches. Let us look at the Bastard's speech in Shakespeare's *King John* (II, i), 'Mad world! mad kings! mad composition!'.

No props or furniture are needed for this speech. It is simple and easy to stage but it is hard to be alone and address the audience. It takes a very relaxed energy to be half a character and half a chorus figure. The Bastard's behaviour is that of a cynical, wryly amused commentator, who has to look after himself, laughing at his own hypocrisy after having been angry and righteous. He is cynical and resigned and wickedly tongue-in-cheek when he mocks his own avarice.

A suitable costume would comprise a plain white shirt and dark trousers (flannel or cord) tucked into boots. You could wear a sweatband around your forehead and have a silk or cotton scarf around your neck. This would provide a certain sense of period, especially if the shirt collar is raised. The sweatband is a practical way of keeping your hair off your face, but also it has a reckless, opportunist quality if you think of it as a badge of allegiance, a mark of the loyalty the Bastard is prepared to trade to the highest bidder.

You could enter upstage right, walking backwards and looking offstage towards the event you have just observed. On reaching centre stage, you could spot the audience, look at them for a moment and then decide to come downstage to talk to them. The first few lines can be an outburst of fury at the behaviour of the two kings and then the following speech can be an explanation, during which you can relax more, smile and divulge your own scheme as part of the 'way the world wags'. At this point you could saunter over to the proscenium arch downstage left and lean against it. The concluding lines gives you back a physical energy with which you can make a swift exit, perhaps centre right.

Say your contemporary speech is Leonidik's 'I loved my mother very much . . .' from Aleksei Arbuzov's *The Promise*. You could keep the shirt, scarf, boots and trousers as you had them for the Shakespeare, but add a short duffel coat or ski jacket and a blue or black sailor-style cap. With the coat collar turned up and the cap and boots, the effect will be ideal for wartime Russia. The sweatband can be removed as the cap can be used to keep your hair off your face.

The setting would be very sparse and simple, so it is important for you to create the atmosphere of a confined space. The movement will have to work within a very narrow focus through eyes and body. You could experiment with restricting yourself to a single chair, using it in a number of ways. You could lean on it, put a foot on it, sit on it forwards or across the back, or sit on the floor and lean against it, grasping hold of it with your arms. If you use a chair the audition must not become an exercise in acting with an item of furniture. Nor should you ignore it. Try to make the focus of Lika and Marek very intimate and close. This will help the claustrophobic atmosphere.

After these two pieces you might have a movement or improvisation session. Now you could remove the cap, scarf, shirt, trousers and boots. Underneath you could be wearing a T-shirt and footless tights. You could then add running shorts or track-suit trousers. The important thing is for the instructor or panel members to see a clear bodyline for the co-ordination exercises. At this point flat feet, knock knees and beer guts will be exposed.

By using three different outfits you will have shown the panel three images of yourself, as yourself and in character, to complement the work you have done.

10. Approaching a Role

If you could learn all there is to know about acting from a book, there would be no need for you to consider going to a drama school. However, I hope that the ideas set out in this chapter will help you in preparing your audition pieces and will spark your talent, intelligence and imagination to find the heart and passion in your chosen speeches.

First of all, read the play for overall sense and an understanding of where your character fits in. Write down your impressions as they occur to you. These will be useful to you later as they are the equivalent of the audience's reactions as it watches the play for the first time, rather than those of an actor who knows the play inside out.

What your friends and acquaintances say about you in real life tells you an enormous amount about how the world in general sees you and often far more about yourself than you can ever be aware of. The same is true of a character in a play. Make a note of everything that the other characters say about your character.

Work out for yourself and write down what you think the reason for your speech is. What is its job in the play? How does it further the story or explain your character? It is part of the 'journey' of the character and must travel somewhere emotionally and practically. Try to assess where your character is at the start of the speech and where he or she is at the end.

Decide where the climax of the speech falls. If one is not apparent, then for the purposes of the audition it may be necessary to invent one aside from the context of the play. If you are to create that clear 'journey' for your character during the course of the speech, then you may have to change the circumstances in which it is delivered.

Before an actor dares to set foot on stage in character, he or she must ask four vital questions:

- Who am I?
- Where am I?

- What am I doing?
- Why am I doing it?

If any of these questions remains unanswered you have no right to take that character on stage in such an unfinished state. The rehearsal process is concerned with answering these questions. Recently I asked a student about a performance choice she had made. She could not explain herself and admitted that she had not read the play beyond her audition speech. It is even worse not to have read the play at all. Such laziness will be apparent to the panel.

Now ask yourself whether your character has any obstacles in his or her path in the 'journey' of the speech. The answer may often seem not very important or dramatic, but you must develop an awareness of the structure of the speech, moment by moment, and looking for the difficulties the character may encounter is a part of that process.

If acting meant simply *becoming* a character on stage, all craft and control would fly out of the window. Imagine what would happen if we took on the role of Richard III! Audiences understand and accept that actors do not really die on stage, or become ill or get injured. So how do you set about establishing that distinction between reality and recreated reality? Over a hundred years ago Coquelin wrote in his book *The Art of the Actor* that an actor playing a character should divide his mind into two parts. Number One (as he called it) plays the role while Number Two is an objective eye, standing outside and monitoring the performance. Number Two might, for instance, notice that a prop is missing or misplaced or that the audience is being inattentive and that Number One should speak up a bit more.

To some extent we split our minds in this way in everyday life. Imagine you are talking to a friend. Even in an intense moment of discussion or argument your mind is able to notice other sounds, smells, etc., without being sidetracked. It may start to rain; you may notice your friend has been eating garlic or is wearing perfume or aftershave you don't like; you may be making a judgement about your friend's clothes or new hairstyle . . . All these things can be going through your mind without affecting the course of your conversation. However, on stage, you might want the audience to be aware of these subtextual reactions and feelings. If you can achieve this, then you will be adding depth to your role. The idea of playing the subtext will be a major element in your work, but it will be very hard for you to work on this alone at this early stage. But do try to be aware of the two parts of your conscious mind and develop a balance between them. Number One must not be allowed to run riot but neither must Number Two be allowed to interfere to the point of stagnation.

You will find some books on acting discuss the dangers of 'demonstrating' your character's emotions to an audience. It is important to understand what is meant by this term. It is used to describe actors who seem to stand outside their roles and watch themselves perform; there appears to be no deep involvement with the character, but a kind of exhibition of the role. This may be due to arrogance or to ignorance. Either way, it shows a basic lack of trust in oneself and in the text of the play.

Do not confuse 'demonstration' with 'representation'. What you are aiming to achieve as an actor is a physical and emotional *representation* of a moment in a character's life, not the actual *presentation* of it. Your job is to communicate these moments by reproducing them. In rehearsal, and sometimes even in performance, you may truly experience the emotions of your scene, but without a conscious control of yourself all the internal emotion in the world is unlikely to affect an audience. It is technique not emotion that will allow you to communicate the intensity of your character's experience to others.

The period of rehearsal is a time of discovery, of experiencing emotions, of experimenting with imaginative ideas and of exploring your speech within the whole life of the play. The performance, whether on stage or for an audition, is concerned with communicating your discoveries, with making your experiences live again for other people.

Finally, a few warnings and ideas to bear in mind as you prepare your speeches.

Don't make your emotions general. Don't cover the whole speech with sadness or drown yourself and the audience with tears for the entire length of your speech. Be specific and place the emotion accurately at the point where it occurs as a result of a particular thought or reaction. Avoid acting the emotional state; go back to the text and ask yourself what is happening, or what has happened, when and how, to cause the character's emotional state.

Don't audition the furniture – or, for that matter, other invisible characters. Don't fall into the trap of trying to create other things and people on stage with you to the detriment of your own performance. After all, it is *you* the panel should be looking at. Some students work so hard with their gestures and their eyes that the panel constantly finds itself concentrating on thin air. You will need to draw attention back to yourself after you have evoked something or someone else. This technique is called 'playing on' or 'playing off' characters or objects.

One way to learn to solve this difficulty is by watching your own behaviour in a real-life situation. Notice how you behave in a group of people, for example as your family prepares a meal. It is very rare for people to stare constantly at each other as they hold a conversation. You will probably find that quite a time goes by without you looking anyone directly in the eye. And you certainly don't stop what you are doing every time you speak in order to look up and get someone's attention.

Take this into the audition situation. If you have to refer to an imaginary character, place them momentarily with your eyes but then bring your eye focus back into your own or another area. This brings the audience's or panel's attention back to you to be redirected where you choose.

One way to rehearse 'playing off' another character is to ask a friend to sit in. Place two chairs back to back, which will make it impossible for you to stare at your partner. Run through the speech and when you feel a particularly strong urge to make contact with the other character, glance in your friend's direction as far as you are able. You will then have to learn to readjust your eye focus so that it doesn't look as if you are gazing at some other object. Try to keep your eye focus within your own imaginative circle. Think of yourself as sitting in a pool of light with the edge of the light being as far as your eyes can focus.

You can extend this exercise by placing your friend in another room, so that you are forced to change the focus into your own environment, at the same time altering your vocal demands because of the distance between you.

The 'fourth wall' of a theatre set is understood by actors and audiences to be invisible so that the action on stage can be seen. You can let your eyes travel through this wall to beyond the panel/audience as far as the back wall of the auditorium. This takes some care as there is a strong distinction between a 'thinking' focus, as the character does not really *see* what he or she is looking at, and the kind of focus that implies something specific is being seen, such as, for instance, a fire on the horizon.

Finally, don't always play the obvious reaction. This is known as 'playing the opposite'. We all sometimes in our lives cover up our real feelings. We pretend that we don't really mind having failed our driving test or whatever and put on a cheery expression to belie the agony and humiliation that we are feeling underneath. If we can show this to an audience, elements of danger and surprise are present and the audience will not be able to relax and make assumptions about a character. By playing in this way, you will also become aware of the pressure of the character's emotional state.

Lisle Jones has been teaching acting and text analysis for 25 years and has added these valuable comments.

The 'acting' component is the core unit of any Theatre Training course. It is here that the work in all other units (voice, movement, text study etc.) is synthesised into an holistic approach to performance. In the first year work should start on the actor himself, sensitising him so that he may respond quickly to stimulus both 'real' and 'imaginary' whilst simultaneously freeing those responses into uninhibited, unselfconscious reaction and expression. At this stage the actor is using only himself; there is no attempt at characterisation, story telling, or interpreting text: it is simply himself in various modes and permutations, any move into characterisation is minimal and relatively unimportant. This groundwork is most important and should not be skimped.

The second stage of the work consists of emphasis on characterisation, analyses of scenes and plays and methods of approaching the same so that intellectual analyses can be transformed into appropriate 'behaviour' at the moment of performance (out of the head and into the body). This work commences and is processed in class exercises and culminates in rehearsed 'production' work approximating as near as possible professional working conditions. For this reason it is very useful if the work in text class can be closely allied to that of the acting class and even better if both subjects can be taught by the same person for it is here that all aspects of the course will finally fuse.

Therefore the wider the acting teacher's experience and knowledge in all the skills of performance the better for all concerned and the more he/she can do to refine the students ultimate thinking *vis-à-vis* performance. The teacher can do this in a consultative capacity in production or if, as is desirable, he/she is a director in their own right, in a fully supervised production.

11. The Craft of Sight-reading

Sight-reading is a vital component of any actor's technique yet constantly directors complain about the lack of skill exhibited at auditions. It seems ironic that the way into finding work should be less skilled than the work itself. After all, without success at an audition, there is no next stage. So why is this particular subject so important?

Many general auditions feature the prepared monologue, rehearsed and memorised perhaps over a long period. However, directors often prefer an actor to read some text of the play in preparation and for a specific role. In this way, a balance of voice, shape and size can be gained more accurately for the final choice.

If your sight-reading skills are poor, it will negate the process for the director and your possible potential will *not* be revealed. Therefore, what makes a good sight-reader? What the process is not about is to prove that you can read aloud – most people can do that already and usually very badly. However, the skills are to do with bringing the text instantly to life with little or sometimes no preparation, by making it sound that it is *not* being read – as in any good radio drama. Therefore, for this you will need experience with a variety of material and have a good understanding of grammar and syntax. You should be fully aware that though we write grammatically in sentences we think in thought phrases and it is those that we need to bring to life from the written page – *not* the sentences. Therefore the action of the mind is revealed through or via the thought phrase. Added to this, the voice requires a flexible and expressive pitch movement to reflect subtle changes of mood and emotion. This requires pacing the text well, giving time for thoughts to be revealed, plus the necessary energy to create and project effectively. Other areas of sight-reading include film tests, television and film commercials, radio drama, voice-overs (e.g. documentaries), post-synchronisation work (e.g. re-recording your own voice), dubbing (e.g. foreign films into

English), recitals (one-person shows or narrations), news reading, auto-cue performance on television, and finally public speaking (e.g. award ceremonies).

Developing sight-reading skills, before you train as an actor, will give you enormous confidence and will help your future career. Experiments with the material offered here will test the condition of your eyesight, the quality of your eye-contact to your audience or another actor, the recognition of word groups as well as the task of learning to relax and read ahead efficiently. The ability to make words live off the page is a rare one and will enable you to move into new creative markets, improving your usefulness and earning capacity in the entertainment industry.

General Auditioning

The audition process is an unsatisfactory one though frequently directors try to improve it. However, time, money and the sheer weight of numbers beating on the doors of employers make it hard to conduct useful and creative sessions. Inevitably the cattle call situation returns where the individual performance feels like a slave being herded towards an area of certain extinction. There is a preference though for an actor to read a specific role in addition to required memorised pieces and often both opportunities are offered to you. Relish the chance and make certain that you can be proficient with the reading opportunity. It will be appreciated as so many actors today are appalling sight-readers and directors despair at their basic lack of skill in a craft industry.

The reading will extend your chances and will afford the director an opportunity to judge your vocal quality in the actual role available, to compare it with other voices he may have heard and to assess a balance between you and the voices of the other characters in the play – rather like balancing the timbre of instruments in an orchestra. Therefore, not only do you need to be at ease whilst reading but available to adapt and be flexible according to the directors' wishes, e.g. Can you be more reflective in this passage? Can your tone of voice be more strident? etc.

The Condition of Your Eyesight
- How good is your eyesight?
- When did you last have your eyes tested?

- Do you wear glasses?
- Should you wear glasses but are too vain in public? (You may have to consider wearing contact lenses in certain circumstances on stage.)
- Can you read small print?
- Can you read well in poor lighting?
- How is your eyesight affected by tiredness or nerves?

If you are not sure about any of these questions, seek professional help from your optician or eye hospital/clinic; weak or lazy eye muscles can be improved easily with exercise.

If you have to wear glasses at an audition for reading only – then, at least, enter without them on. As you take yourself into the scene, bring out the glasses perhaps as part of the character, so that, instead of thinking of your glasses as a block, use them as a character choice and as an extension to your arm and hand – a useful prop. You could have a wide choice, from the studious lecturer who peers over the top of his glasses perched on the end of his nose to the irate newspaper editor who constantly pushes them up onto his forehead – with all the combinations in between.

Whatever you decide on, your glasses must never get in the way. Practise removing them easily and frequently so that you never remain lost behind them. In effect, this is the beginning of your rehearsal and part of your job as an actor.

Training Your Eye Muscles

If you have serious problems your optician or the eye clinic can give you a series of exercises to strengthen and balance both eyeballs. However, as a check and general toning up before an audition – try this one.

- Hold a pencil tip upright two feet (60 cm) away from your face.
- Focus your eyes on the tip as you bring it closer to and level with your nose.
- The image will go out of focus but it must not double, becoming two tips. If that occurs then one eye ball has given up and jumped away to the right or left.
- Working with a partner to observe the movement of your eyeballs, strain to hold on to the image, as this will strengthen both eye muscles and generally improve sharpness of vision.

- This applies particularly today if you have been watching television or staring at your personal computer. Your eyes will need adjusting before reading aloud and this is the exercise to do just that.

I was given the above exercise many years ago at St George's Hospital in London. I was finding great difficulty in learning lines as my right eye ached very quickly with close study and then I found it hard to concentrate. The improvement was dramatic alongside many other exercises for my specific weak eye-muscle condition.

Soon after I was watching an old 'B' movie on television and noticed an army general standing at his office window doing the same pencil exercise whilst talking to his subaltern. I discovered later that this had long been an old army trick for toning up the eyes before rifle practice. They called it 'Getting your eye in'.

Confidence and losing your place

Sit in front of a mirror – with good lighting and a book of any sort but with reasonable sized print. The passage of Dickens opposite will serve as a good example. Begin reading aloud and at any suitable point – stop, look up into the reflection of your eyes, refocus if necessary, then let your eyes drop back to the book and continue reading, repeating the eye contact three or four times.

You will find that *if* as you look up at yourself in to the mirror, you *don't* move your head or the book (i.e. only your eyeballs move) you will return to the last word you read *thereby* not losing your place. Although this may seem unnaturally restrictive, it does prove that if you are nervous and unsure of a text, there is a way of guaranteeing not losing your place. This will give you immense confidence in the privacy of your own rehearsal or amongst friends, until such time as you can free up into a more natural form of eye contact.

- You may find it hard to keep your head still when you make eye contact. Try it out with a friend to see how well you can control your head/neck relationship as you look up from a script.
- You may also allow the script to drop downwards or swing to the side as you look up. The catastrophe here is doubled, for as you bring your eyes down on to the script again, the script is travelling in either the opposite direction or creating a zigzag train crash for the eyes to try and refocus in.

Example text

A dark and dreary night; people nestling in their beds or circling late about the fire; Want, colder than Charity, shivering at the street corners; church towers humming with the faint vibrations of their own tongues, but newly resting from the preachment 'One'! The earth covered with a sable pall as for the burial of yesterday; the clumps of dark trees, its giant plumes of funeral feathers, waving sadly to and fro: all hushed, all noiseless, and in deep repose, save the swift clouds that skim across the moon, and the cautious wind as, creeping after them upon the ground, it stops to listen, and goes rustling on, and stops again, and follows, like a savage on the trail.

Whither go the clouds and wind, so eagerly? If, like guilty spirits they repair to some dread conference with powers like themselves, in what wild regions do the elements hold council, or where unbend in terrible disport?

CHARLES DICKENS

Learning to phrase

Use a well-written piece of narrative prose to begin with as conversation/dialogue and character choice doesn't help until you've mastered basic principles. Again in front of a mirror, though preferably to family or friends, commence reading out loud. At each punctuation mark STOP reading completely – look up into the mirror, or your partner's eyes, make proper eye contact in focus, then look down again and proceed with the reading until you reach the next full stop, comma, question mark etc.

You will find this irritating and perhaps unnaturally slow. However, it will prove the following points to you.

- With well-constructed prose and by observing all the punctuation – it will at least be well phrased into proper sense groups.
- You will not lose your place – keeping your head and script still as before.
- You will be forced to slow down – most people read too quickly.
- You will find time to read ahead.
- You will have more time to make sense of the text.
- You will find time to improve your expression, colour and rhythm of speech.

You must remember that for the sake of communication on paper the educated world writes in grammatical sentences. As human beings we think and speak in thought phrases, which may or may not make up to a sentence. Therefore, if you try to read back the printed text in sentences to your audience, you will not discover the moment by moment journey of the author's ideas. Your result will be academic and lifeless.

Example text

But, there were deep green patches in the growing corn at first, that people looked at awfully. Year after year they re-appeared; and it was known that underneath those fertile spots, heaps of men and horses lay buried, indiscriminately enriching the ground. The husbandmen who ploughed those places, shrunk from the great worms abounding there; and the sheaves they yielded, were, for many a long year, called the Battle Sheaves, and set apart; and no one ever knew a Battle Sheaf to be among the last load at a Harvest Home. For a long time, every furrow that was turned, revealed some fragments of the fight. For a long time, there were wounded trees upon the battle-ground; and scraps of hacked and broken fence and wall, where deadly struggles had been made; and trampled parts where not a leaf or blade would grow. For a long time, no village girl would dress her hair or bosom with the sweetest flower from that field of death: and after many a year had come and gone, the berries growing there, were still believed to leave too deep a stain upon the hand that plucked them.

The Seasons in their course however, though they passed as lightly as the summer clouds themselves, obliterated, in the lapse of time, even these remains of the old conflict; and wore away such legendary traces of it as the neighbouring people carried in their minds, until they dwindled into old wives' tales, dimly remembered round the winter fire, and waning every year. Where the wild flowers and berries had so long remained upon the stem untouched, gardens arose, and houses were built, and children played at battles on the turf. The wounded trees had long ago made Christmas logs, and blazed and roared away. The deep green patches were no greener now than the memory of those who lay in dust below.

The Battle of Life CHARLES DICKENS

Reading Ahead – 1

- Again with a mirror or partner – read a new passage out aloud – but this time only search for the FULL STOPS. When you see one approaching, test how far ahead you can make eye contact whilst completing speaking the sentence. If you can manage four or five words you are doing well.
- Hold the eye contact in focus long enough to register a thought from the sense of the text. Too short an eye contact – a glance in fact, becomes a comment on the individual or a lack of confidence on your part really to commit yourself to what you're saying. Too long a look provokes again a subtextual reference to the other individual and could be read as a stare, again which has no reference to the text necessarily.

The trap of this exercise is that whilst you are busy trying to find the full stops and thinking about reading ahead, the actual vocal expression becomes dull and flat and the phrasing of the previous exercise disappears. Tape your efforts and listen carefully to the varying results between all these exercises.

Reading Ahead – 2

- Repeat the exercise above, but this time when you look up, test whether you can remember and speak any of the following sentence before looking back to your script.
- This exercise is a real challenge but excellent for forcing you to stretch your eyes further across the page.

The trap in this exercise is that the end of the first sentence and the beginning of the next might sound the same as you try to hold two images in your mind at once. Try to change your tone of voice between the two sentences so that the thoughts are separated.

Summary

- Once you feel comfortable with phrase structure within the grammar of the sentence and in a wide variety of material – relax and read naturally using your own instinct to choose the appropriate moment to look up from the script.
- Reading to yourself silently and reading aloud have nothing in common. The pace and method of processing imagery in your brain silently is not to be compared to telling a story out aloud, where your listeners cannot see the written word.

The audience has to process the imagery from your vocal texture. If you rush that for them they will not have time to establish any images.

- The eye works like a camera and your brain recognises words and phrases as photographic shapes. The more you read the more photographs your brain can store. Phrases such as 'As far as I'm concerned . . .', 'After a while . . .', are not normally read word by word. They can be picked up and processed as a group thereby speeding up your comprehension and delivery.
- Working with difficult constructions in language is an important test of your ability. Charles Dickens and George Bernard Shaw offer you elegant but very long sentences with complicated parenthesis to negotiate. They will certainly teach you how to unravel the phrase from the sentence. After you've conquered them, everything else will be far easier by comparison.

PART III

The Actor's Training

12. Pre-Drama School Training

During years 11 and 12 at secondary school you will be faced with a wide range of choices. If your heart is set on a theatre career via a recognised drama school, then you may well be interested in one of the excellent pre drama school options.

The BTEC National Diplomas in performing arts are now offered by many further education colleges for 16–18-year-olds. These are two-year courses, equivalent in standard to A Levels, and normally requiring four GCSEs at grade C for entry. They are vocationally and practically based, and are viewed very favourably by drama schools because of the practical training which they offer.

In response to government policy the National Council For Vocational Qualifications (NCVQ) have introduced a new range of vocational qualifications – the GNVQ. These new awards, available at two levels, are being phased in over the next few years to replace the BTEC first and National Diplomas. You should check with your parents, teachers and career officer what the best option for you may be. For information in your area of available courses contact your local careers service office.

The two colleges described below have a particular significance for the performing arts.

Stratford-upon-Avon College

The Willows North, Alcester Road, Stratford-upon-Avon, Warwickshire CV37 9QR, Tel: 01789 266245

This college has an international reputation as a centre for drama, theatre and media studies. It has direct links with Coventry University and is actively supported by the Royal Shakespeare Company. You will find that you are involved in rigorous academic, practical and creative studies whether you are working for

GCSE A Levels or a BTEC qualification. The drama and theatre programmes are physically and intellectually demanding and will provide you with an excellent preparation for entry into the world of theatre, television, music, art and education. You will be encouraged to take responsibility for managing your own learning programme which will include workshop activities, seminars, group work, lectures and supported self-study. You will be asked to work with others to write, design, perform and direct theatrical events, during which you will share the responsibility for the conduct of both performers and audience.

Courses offered are:

1-year GCSE Drama and Media Arts
Drama A Level Programme
1-year Drama and Theatre Studies, post-A Level
2-year BTEC National Diploma in Performing Arts
2-year BTEC Higher National Diploma in Performing Arts, Theatre practice

The British Record Industry Trust (BRIT)

Performing Arts and Technology School, 60 The Crescent, Croydon CR0 2HN, Tel: 0181-665 5242, Fax: 0181-665 5197

This is a unique state school, independent of any local education authority and all places are free. The school is designed for students aged 14–19 who wish to acquire a broad, balanced education with specialisation in performing arts, media and associated technology. The facilities include a purpose-built arts building housing a 500-seat performance centre, music laboratory and practice rooms, dance studios, technology suite, box office, radio broadcast suite, television studio and editing facility, and a music recording studio.

Courses offered include:

City and Guilds – 1 year in TV, video and radio production; AS/A Levels in film studies, media, performing arts and theatre studies.
BTEC National Diploma — business and finance – entertainment industry, media, performing arts.
Higher National Certificate and Diploma — TV, film and video production.
National Vocational Qualifications – NVQ and GNVQ in business, media and management (year 14 only).

Most of the major drama schools such as RADA, LAMDA and Central will focus on you and your acting process in a highly concentrated manner. The two years prior to that can be of enormous advantage to you giving you the skills and language of professional theatre, film and television beforehand plus the chance to learn ancillary skills that may not be available to you in the 3-year course – for example front-of-house, box office, make-up, stage management, lighting etc. This completing of the process in production will add a healthy respect from your future fellow workers as well.

13. Your Drama School Course

It would take several books to cover all the subjects contained in a three-year training. There are several excellent books available on most aspects of your studies, some of which I have listed under Further Reading at the end of this book.

A good library of your own is vital to your study and understanding of what you are learning and discovering. The more books you have, the likelier it is that you will be able to find something pertinent to what you have just experienced in class. Reading something written by someone else will give you another way of looking at it and help you assimilate your course content.

Acting

In Further Reading you will find several excellent books on acting which are used by many teachers and schools as the basis of or as a supplement to their own acting courses. Each school has its own particular approach and combination of tried and tested projects to complement any written theory. I set out below a typical first-term acting course to give you some idea of what to expect. All the other subjects would interlink with the acting course, and the voice, movement and singing courses would be designed to support the various acting projects.

First year – first term

The first week of orientation culminates in a presentation of all the new students' original audition monologues given as a 'staged performance' in the academy theatre. This is seen by staff and other students only as an introduction to the school. The new students' group is asked to organise the performance themselves, introduce it in any way they see fit and to add any group item they can organise and rehearse in the time available. This is the beginning of the creation of a sense of ensemble: the group is obliged to co-operate at the earliest opportunity. After the show there is a party for staff and new students to relax and socialise with each other.

During the first five weeks of acting classes a major classical text, such as Shakespeare or a Jacobean play, is rehearsed by the acting tutor without props, costume or scenery as a 'discovery play'. The result, however rough and ready, is shown to the other staff and then followed by a critique session. The object of this exercise is to underline the need for training and to help the staff judge the needs of the group as a whole and the needs of individual students. It gives the new student an idea of how far he or she has to go and creates an opportunity for specific problems, particulary in the areas of voice and movement, to be pointed out at an early stage.

The sixth week is a production week and all formal classes are cancelled. The first-year students develop a movement project or collage with music from work begun in movement classes directed by their movement tutor. No speech is used so that concentration can remain on the body and again staff members can spot and analyse specific difficulties at this early stage before bad habits become fixed.

During the second half of the first term, acting exercises are introduced into the syllabus. These are taken from the work of Stanislavsky and allow the actor to explore him- or herself and develop imaginative and sensory skills without relying on props, costume or furniture. Solo work leads gradually to two- or three-person group work.

The last week of term is another project or performance week for the whole school. The first-year students rehearse all day a self-devised group improvisation using both movement and the spoken word, guided by their acting tutor.

So the work continues, term by term, monitored by the entire staff every six weeks to assess student development and the areas of greatest need for the next block of work.

Voice

The importance placed on voice studies varies greatly from school to school. It can be a sensitive area to approach as it engages with the established personality of the individual student perhaps more than any other aspect of the training. We have all been using our voice from the beginning of our lives and feel very protective towards its identity. Unlike learning to tap dance or play the violin, it is not a skill we acquire deliberately; we already know how to speak – well or badly – and we have been doing it for a long time. To be told to start learning the skill from scratch all over again can feel like an affront.

The diction of plays written only thirty years ago can seem fairly foreign to us now. The majesty and emotional grandeur of Shakespeare's words or the precise, amusing and overstressed richness of Restoration comedy can be very tricky to make understandable without a conscious awareness of the ways in which our voices can be used.

Voice studies are divided into 'voice' itself, how the physical instrument works within the mind and body of the individual, and 'speech', the use to which that instrument is put in the articulation of sound. Most schools now recognise the important connection between voice and movement. The Alexander Technique, or a physical discipline such as T'ai Chi or Feldenkrais, seem necessary to rectify the problems brought about by modern casual posture. There are so many demands and stresses placed on young people today that voice studies cannot really begin until these major tensions have been released.

Standard English or Received Pronunciation (RP) is a bugbear to be faced by every new intake. RP should ideally be looked on as just another accent that you can acquire without losing your own identity, rhythm or local colour. You will need it if you are to play in works by Shaw, Coward or Wilde, for instance. However, 'a bad sound is a bad sound is a bad sound' and it is vital to rid your voice of any unpleasant sounds or any accent or dialect that cannot be understood because, to take one example, of a constricted placement due to personal tension unrelated to the accent itself.

Depending on the school's syllabus, you might learn phonetics, verse-speaking, sight-reading, accents and dialects, radio technique, voice-over and post-synchronisation. These will all be extra to your basic training.

A good singing technique will help you understand placement and breathing if the staff make a strong correlation between the spoken and the sung word. The presence of an Alexander teacher at a singing tutorial can provide a wonderfully effective short cut to an understanding of the support needs of performance and the release of unnecessary tension in the body and the vocal mechanism.

In the booklist, Further Reading, you will find several excellent voice books, which will be vital to your training and your own personal library. The drama schools follow similar structures in their voice courses as these books, and your voice studies will relate directly to your work in other subjects such as verse, acting, singing and textwork. You will thus be enabled to apply what you are learning in your voice classes to other areas of study and receive feedback from a variety of staff members. It is useful for your voice tutor to see how you translate the work you do together into other classes, where the combination is not primarily on the voice.

Movement

Your movement studies will help you cope with the varied demands of, say, a contemporary drama, a stylised Restoration comedy or the earthy physicality of a Lorca play. Greek drama often provides a good starting point as the actor is required to match the scale and emotion of the verse. It pushes back the boundaries of mind, body and voice and allows the actor to test himself against the material and set his or her own limitations in perspective. This can be an exciting project, particularly if the text is accompanied by rhythmically sensuous and vibrant percussion instruments to support the ensemble chorus.

The object of teaching movement is to find a way, through the use of text and through exercises, of getting in touch with your own body, of understanding it and of making it expressive. The aim is to adopt a complete body language that will eventually speak for itself without the need for words. 'Belonging to the earth' is one of the first vital steps towards achieving a 'centring' of the body dynamic, allowing the natural flow from mind to body to voice, short-circuiting the social and physical inhibitions that our so-called modern society inflicts so readily.

In Chapter 14, 'Movement and the Student Actor', Brigitte Kelly, a long-standing colleague of mine, sets out her personal perspective on the teaching of movement.

14. Movement and the Student Actor

Brigitte Kelly

Towards the end of my dancing career, I first took part in, and later choreographed and directed, quite a few pantomimes and summer seasons. It was really then that I encountered a cross-section of the profession, including singers, actors and comedians. Confronted with the task of making them not only move but dance, I had to search around for a totally different approach from the normally intolerant one of the ballet person. I made quite a few mistakes at first. I gave movements that were too complicated and provoked resistance to my efforts. Imagine trying to get the huge, immovable Tommy Cooper to take part in a dance routine; he was charming, but literally could not tell his right leg from his left. There was often hostility towards the 'dance person', and I realised that these non-dancers were simply protecting themselves, and the bigger the 'star' the less they co-operated, with the exception of Bruce Forsyth who of course is an excellent dancer.

Later I ran free movement classes for literally all-comers. I grew to love these classes and by taking the human element into account I think those 'amateurs' taught me to teach. Among them were student and working actors. I liked the way they asked questions, took such trouble over detail, thought out what they were doing, and the way they would stand in front of the mirror, anxiously whispering, 'Is that right?' Regrettably not the normal reaction of dancers. The questions stimulated me to find answers, and from there it seemed a natural progression to take 'actors' movement' as a separate subject.

The Body

Ideally each person should be treated individually with private coaching, though a class has the advantage, with less focus of attention on one individual, of giving the actor a certain degree of anonymity in which to experiment and overcome natural embarrassment. Also the individual personality has to conform to the overall personality of the class, and that is not a bad thing. Individual problems can be dealt with after the class is over, but the safety of the herd produces an unselfconscious climate for work, and once the actor has understood the nature of concerted work, the results can be excellent – always providing, of course, the person is willing to learn and take advice, above all to work physically far beyond what he or she believes are his or her limitations.

General Advice

Generally speaking, men, Anglo-Saxon *men*, are rather tightly strung together. The damp and cold of our climate makes for stiff-jointed people, with incipient rheumatism! There is a certain type of physique – thin, taut and usually coupled with a lot of tension – that finds dance movement extremely difficult. We all have to work with the equipment we have, and not strive to add to the strain by becoming frustrated with ourselves. A calm mind is the first step to a relaxation of tension and the easing of muscular tension of the wrong sort. Work with what you've got, not with what you wish you had! A very loose-limbed, supple body needs tightening up; a stiff one needs loosening up. Treat the body as your instrument; don't take correction personally, be humble, drop your ego. There is no place for conceit, smugness or self-satisfaction as you will have to go on learning all your working life. Keep the channel open.

Classical Ballet

There is a certain prejudice among some academy directors and principals against classical ballet. This may be a lack of understanding of the value of the basic training. Certainly ballet is often seen in terms of strained neck muscles or of a restricted diaphragm causing a small breathy voice. This last is due to the intensive feats of endurance that are demanded of today's dancer, and of course the dancer is never required to speak, therefore the voice is in most cases undeveloped.

The early stages of simple exercises at the *barre* are based on the posture, modes and manners of our ancestors all of whom walked a great deal more than we do, and the upper classes rode horses as a matter of course. The classical basic exercises are isolation exercises, of the foot, the leg, the arms and the use of the head. No attempt should be made by the teacher to produce a classical dancer and there should be no overstretching. It is ridiculous to expect an actor to execute a *glissade* or a *pas de chat*. However, a centring for balance is essential, including some springing and free movement. But beware, ballet is like knowledge – a little is dangerous.

The Importance of the Back

A strong back is of primary importance for every human being. The Western way of life takes us further and further away from the strong stance and upright carriage of past generations. At last young people are becoming aware of this, hence the proliferation of health clubs. However, there are strong reservations against violent exercises for the untrained body. A lot of harm can be done by aerobics classes and the various outrageously athletic classes that take money from unsuspecting enthusiasts.

The careful, supervised development of the back muscles is a must for anyone entering the theatre. If the back is strong, it supports the entire stance and leaves the neck, hands and arms free for expression. Body-building programmes are good, especially work on the special body-control machines, particularly if they are supervised by an ex-dancer. Men, beware of weightlifting, which will build up enormous muscles and create great vocal tension. Swimming is excellent, especially the breast stroke which opens the lungs, expands the rib-cage and develops a breathing pattern to support future voice exercises.

Good posture must be lived, inside and outside the studio. It should become a habit. The sloppy stance of the be-jeaned young is something that can be easily imitated by the actor if required, but before you can slouch you have to learn good posture and balance. The present fashion for sneakers with thick rubber soles tends to minimise sensitivity in the muscles of the soles of the feet. Leather soles or bare feet are preferable in class, and the actor would do well to wear leather-soled shoes at all times to continue the balance achieved in class. On the whole women have less of a problem as they tend to wear lighter shoes.

The habitual clothes for a general movement class should always be figure-hugging, plain and warm. It is essential for the instructor to be able to see the outline of the physique. Of the other sports, tennis, fencing and running are good. Horse-riding creates bad movement resulting in awkwardness in walking (think of John Wayne). The clasping of the flanks of the horse with the inside thigh develops the wrong muscles.

Period Movement

How can we imitate our ancestors if we do not know how they looked and what conditioned the way they moved and behaved? Any would-be actor should read domestic history, spend hours in picture galleries, study costumes and furniture in the wonderful museums, which are within most people's reach. Study these historical figures and imagine how you would manipulate that voluminous skirt around that tiny pedestal table without knocking it over. Throw the bedspread around your shoulders and manipulate it in front of the mirror. Put on a pair of tight-fitting pants, gentlemen; are you holding the muscles of your buttocks in or do they wobble when you walk? Girls, tie the bedspread around your waist and then walk backwards! Have a good look at the old ladies and gentlemen of the upper middle classes, they're a dying breed in more ways than one. Study books of photographs of the past out of the library; there are plenty of them nowadays. *Self-help*: do it for yourself! Use your own brain   it's cheaper! Remember that our clothes were influenced by the times in which people lived – and they still are. The liberated movements of the 1920s and 1930s are in total contrast to the corseted, stiff stance of the Elizabethans, etc.

Television, studied intelligently, is a wonderful educator for the aspiring actor. The authenticity of the costumes and sets, not to mention the actors' movements, is most impressive, particularly in period productions. Study and imitate with the analytical and discerning eye of the nascent professional. Use video recordings for prolonged study. We have wonderful actors — learn from them.

15. What Is Expected of You

Acting, voice and movement, three subjects discussed in Chapter 13, are only the tip of a very large iceberg of a course that may include as many as thirty-six separate subjects over the three-year period. It is an exciting prospect.

How are you going to handle the stress of the hard work and being under close scrutiny all day long for five or six days a week? Personal relationships, within or outside your group, can add extra pressure and distract you from your work. It is inevitable that you will go through phases of loving some fellow students or members of staff, or hating them, or simply being bored by them. You are in an intense and competitive environment, but it is all part and parcel of the life you will lead as a professional actor.

Attitude

How you cope with these personal problems will depend very much on your attitude and emotional state. Meeting all the requirements of learning assignments, background reading, general research and exercises is asking a lot. If all you want to do is just get by, then you have only your own conscience to deal with until the day you get thrown out.

This chapter deals with the kind of behaviour that is expected of you and the way most schools operate. It should be clear to you whether you have the right sort of attitude to adapt to a world of self-discipline which is very different from the style of discipline imposed by parents and school. I have come across many students who admit that they wasted most of their first year at drama school because they could not adapt to this new way of working until it was almost too late.

Class Conduct

Most days will consist of trying to take in enormous amounts of new information without having the time to digest it, use it or even understand it. It is vital to develop an efficient note-taking technique. A separate file for each subject might be a good idea. (Not all the subjects will need notes.) You could consider long-hand, shorthand, speedwriting or cassettes. Make sure staff allow you enough time to take down important points as there will be no opportunity to catch up later and you will probably forget or remember inaccurately if you trust your memory alone. Staff members might be excellent theatre people but they might not be very experienced teachers. Help them to teach you by encouraging them to go at a speed you can follow and make time to discuss areas you don't understand.

Attendance

A hundred per cent attendance is compulsory. You will be told on your first day that the only acceptable excuse for absence is if you are dying or dead. The joke is serious. Feeling sick, tired or whatever is simply not good enough. In one day you could miss the realisation and information that might mean a giant leap forward for you; you might miss the one singing exercise that will unlock your throat tension. If you do have to miss a class, ask a fellow student for notes and check with the staff members concerned. Don't try to catch up in the next class as staff and students will now be involved in something else.

Punctuality

Be early rather than on time, and never ever be late. There is nothing worse in a creative training programme than being disturbed once a session is under way. Most teachers forbid late entry and simply lock the door. In any case you will want to prepare and adjust for each class. It is not a question of merely turning up and waiting to be fed information. Forget your school environment; here 50 per cent of class input is down to the students.

Preparation

Most classes will require you to have done some preparation, for instance to have learned a sonnet or perfected a dance routine. If the work is unprepared the only loser is you. It is always apparent to staff and fellow students when work is ill-prepared. If you become lax, then you won't survive the course. Sometimes you might get away with it and come up with some wonderful piece of imaginative work without thought or preparation. But you are a fool if you think you can rely on luck or inspiration alone.

You may often be irritated by fellow students being ill-prepared and seeming to get away with it time and time again. It can affect your own work, hold up your own development and be a drain on your emotions. If speaking to the guilty party has no effect, you may have to take the matter to the student council or your group tutor. You would do well to sort the matter out for yourself. You will meet the same problem as a professional actor and then you will have no authority to appeal to. Do your best to avoid picking up your fellow students' bad habits, stick to what you believe in and try to maintain your own integrity.

Daily Organisation

Your training is going to produce an actor that audiences will want to pay to see. The investment of money, time and energy needed to achieve that end result is almost incalculable. Part of the initial training is in the economic use of your time and energy.

As well as your note files for the subjects requiring written work, keep a 'sacred' notebook for the timetable, names and telephone numbers and a dated order of required homework. It is impossible to remember everything with the tremendous rate of work done and experienced. You are likely to lose track of time: a week can easily seem like two days when you are so busy.

Keep all your equipment and reference books in your personal locker, so that everything you may need for a class is readily available. To make an efficient and creative contribution to each class you will need to keep a note of when you require tap shoes, movement outfits, ballet shoes, music scores, scripts, props and so on, when you need to have obtained material from the library and chased up research references, when scenes should have been learned and rehearsed by.

There is nothing more infuriating than to find the book you need desperately is out on loan to a student who is away sick or that you have lent your tap shoes to a fellow student who has mislaid his locker key and cannot retrieve them in time for your class. These things happen over and over again and what a waste of time they are for everyone.

The pressure is real and exciting and you will need time to unwind. Parties and late nights may seem a very attractive aspect of your new-found freedom, but keep them for the weekend so that you aren't bringing your morning-afters into class with you.

Group Behaviour

The golden rule is to treat others as you would wish to be treated yourself, even if they don't always return the compliment. Work with everyone in your group; don't play safe by always working with a particular chum. Your development will be limited if you are over-familiar with a partner who will let you get away with less challenging work. You will also fall into the trap of anticipating each other's reactions, which makes for very tame work.

You won't like everyone, but the work has to come first. I realise that is easier for me to write than for you to do. But think, for the rest of your career you could be cast in plays with people you don't like, respect or admire and you could find yourself working with directors who are less than helpful. You might as well get used to it now. Three years can be a long time to avoid someone in your acting group.

Syllabus

Some schools are still very *ad hoc* when it comes to their teaching staff, equipment and syllabus. Most, though, have developed an overall plan over many years of experience than can be adapted to fit the needs of any particular group of students. While you are undergoing your very expensive period of study, it is as well to know what that overall plan is and the reason for everything that you are asked to do. After years teaching the same subject, tutors can forget that they need to explain the purpose behind exercises. Be polite, but don't follow blindly hoping it will all make sense in the end. Sometimes, of course, a staff member will deliberately not explain the point of an exercise, so that the class comes to it with no preconceptions. That still needs spelling out for you.

It is important for you to understand how the different subjects fit together. Don't worry if you hear the same thing said in three or four different subject classes. Certain concepts need reiterating over and over again and it is good to have these ideas expressed in slightly different ways by different members of staff. For instance, you might understand immediately what is meant by 'working from your centre' but it might still take a year or more for you to put that understanding into practice. Part of the responsibility of the group is to be patient with each other, particularly with those who are slower to grasp ideas, and to help each other to catch up without being patronising.

Research

It is to be hoped that you will have access to a good library during your studies to help you in your research on plays, speeches, costumes, period manners and so on. Your own library is a valuable part of your investment, so use your Christmas and birthday lists wisely! It is worth hunting around secondhand bookshops for theatre books and plays as well as remaindered art books, which provide useful picture references. Postcards from museums and galleries are handy too. Many galleries sell special-ised handbooks on costume construction, patterns, make-up and jewellery.

The two major theatre collections in England are held at the Theatre Museum, National Museum of the Performing Arts in Covent Garden, London and the Mander and Mitchenson Theatre Collection in Beckenham, Kent. Both are willing to help with serious inquiries for research, but make sure you know exactly what you are looking for before you waste their valuable time. Enclose a stamped addressed envelope if you are submitting a written query. There are also specialist collections on music-hall and pantomime, etc., which may not necessarily be open to members of the public although the theatre museums might be prepared to put you in touch by letter. You might also find your local theatre and any actors you know are happy to help you with your researches.

In Chapter 16, 'Minimum Requirements', Prunella Scales dis-cusses the actor's training from a personal viewpoint. It is a very clear statement of the responsibilities of the actor. Miss Scales is an experienced teacher as well as a fine actress and trained at the Old Vic School which was founded by Michel Saint-Denis. That was probably the most ideally complete programme ever devised and many schools, the world over, have used Saint-Denis's ideas as the basis for their courses. Miss Scales's notes, which have been revised for this book, were originally presented to the Arts Council Training Panel in 1979. I am most grateful to her for permission to reprint her wise (and utopian) thoughts here.

16. Minimum Requirements

Prunella Scales

These are some notes I first made in 1979 on the minimum that I (as an actress or as a director) would expect an actor about to leave drama school to have learned also perhaps what, as the parent of a student myself, I would hope to find in drama training.

Technical

Vocal
A reasonably free and flexible speaking voice; an acquaintance with his or her own particular vocal problems and the ability and knowledge to work on them; a constantly growing range and control; an ability to speak 'standard English' and competence in at least one regional dialect. I would not insist on a foreign language, but the ability to read phrases correctly in German, French, Italian, Latin, Spanish, etc., is helpful.

I think any student leaving drama school should be a competent sight-reader in both verse and prose, and that any student with particular difficulty in this area should have been given special coaching and extra practice.

Musical
Ability to sing chorally, hold a part in simple harmony, sight-read a simple melody line, and play at least one instrument 'a bit'.

Physical
Main problems dealt with (special tensions, weaknesses, self-consciousness, etc.); the ability and knowledge to work on any minor problems that persist.

Ability to take simple dance routines from a professional choreographer, also (especially actors) simple fight routines in sabre, rapier and foil, and modern unarmed combat, from a professional fight arranger; also simple gymnastic routines from a professional tumbler.

A good standard of health and a sense of responsibility over it; ability to cope cheerfully and unobtrusively with illness, colds, hangovers, etc.

A trained actor should have been taught dances of (at least) the medieval, Elizabethan, Restoration, eighteenth-, nineteenth- and twentieth-century periods.

Costume and make-up

All trained actors and actresses should have had experience in the wearing of (at least) medieval, Elizabethan, Restoration, eighteenth-, nineteenth- and early twentieth-century costumes. They should know where to go to find pictures of these periods, and have an actor's approach to the whole question of costume: how was it worn? why? how would *this* particular character wear it? They should be able to make up appropriately to a costume or character, and be competent in the appropriate dressing of their own hair and wigs. (Personally I think they also should know how to clean and dress their own wigs, but that is being exigent.)

Mechanical media

Every drama student should have the experience of playing in front of a camera or cameras and the opportunity to see the result. Video equipment now seems to me essential in drama schools. I do not myself believe one can teach 'camera technique' – it should be enough to give students the chance to work with cameras and to see themselves and each other on screen afterwards. In the same way, I do not believe in the mystique of 'radio technique', but of course every student should have the opportunity to work and experiment with microphones, and to hear the results played back to the class. Wisely handled, this need not make them self-conscious and tricksy; ideally it should make them unself-conscious and daring in the mechanical media.

Backstage experience

I think it is *very* important to train actors, directors, designers and stage-managers *together*, at least in the same building, and sharing some classes. I don't believe in pampering the acting course, so I would hope all acting students would have some experience of backstage work, perhaps during their first year by working on the final showings of the previous year, as assistant stage managers, stage crew, scene-painters and dressers, etc.

(This is just one of the arguments for decent, though not necessarily purpose-built, premises for drama schools, with constant access to a properly equipped theatre.)

Non-Technical

General theatrical education
Different students have different educational gaps. I believe that drama students should be taught and encouraged to visit, in their own time and at their own expense (though, of course, there should be substantial student concessions), theatres (regional and commercial, classical and fringe), operas, musicals, circus, clubs and films of all styles and periods.

I think they should be reasonably well-read by the time they leave drama school in Shakespeare, Restoration comedy, Ibsen, Chekhov and Wilde, as well as in a representative number of twentieth-century playwrights from all over the world. A drama school should encourage students to continue this reading throughout their working lives, and to back it with poetry, novels, biography, history, and short stories of all periods. Every drama school should have a library of such books.

I believe it quite important that a working actor should be aware of current affairs, both political and social, worldwide and local, but this is perhaps outside the scope of drama training.

General behaviour
The well-trained actor should be punctual, reasonably sober, polite, friendly, respectful, though not sycophantic, towards directors and older artists, quiet and attentive at rehearsals, and word-perfect when required.

When called on to understudy, he should have been trained to be at all his principal's rehearsals, unless specially asked not to by the director or company manager, and know all the lines and business well *before* the first night. (The final dress rehearsals are often the time when voices give out and the accidents happen, and the understudies may be needed.)

The well-trained actor should behave with unfailing courtesy to all staff, whether stage, wardrobe, theatre or studio, and understand the practical and professional advisability of this.

The job of acting

Clive Swift's book, *The Job of Acting*, should be required reading in all drama schools.

There should be lectures on the economics of acting – salaries, national insurance, income tax, the advisability or necessity for savings, insurance policies and so on. An Equity officer should visit drama students in their final term to speak about the union.

When they finally get Equity cards, well-trained ex-students should know and care enough about their profession to read all circulated union literature (however daunting) and exercise their vote when called on. (Most of the bad conditions and much of the hardship in the profession today are due to the general apathy of the Equity membership.)

A Personal View

I haven't mentioned improvisation, masks, or work on animals. All these were enormously helpful in my own training, but I don't know of many teachers qualified to do such work. I think perhaps I *would* expect a drama graduate to have worked on various forms of improvisation, but not, unless he was lucky, to have worked on masks, animals, etc., and only if he was *very* lucky, to have found a teacher who could really help.

This brings me to the vital question, well outside the scope of 'Minimum Expectations': how exactly do you teach *acting*? In England, we usually teach acting on a 'have-a-bash', hit-or-miss system: 'I got a lot from Mr So-and-So'; 'Oh, I couldn't bear him, but I found Miss Thing a great help.'

I deplore this system, like Sydney Smith's Yorkshire, as a very great evil: one *can* teach talented actors to act better, and one can teach less talented actors to act well, or at least correctly. In a Peter Gill production, for instance, you will see both phenomena. But in very few drama schools will you find teachers who know the magic formula. It really *is* a formula, though it can be expressed in many different terms, and does not depend on 'charisma' or 'personality' or 'rapport' or any of the other vague have-a-bashery hit-or-miss terms. And in even fewer drama schools will you find an entire staff who understand and believe in such a formula, and who work together to promulgate it.

Indeed, I suspect there are few drama schools where the staff meet together at all at regular intervals to co-ordinate their ideas and discuss their students in a constructive way.

(I shall be attacked for the terms 'correctly' and 'magic formula' but I'm prepared to defend and explain them to anyone who has half-an-hour to spare!)

It has been frequently said that drama schools should bring in working actors and directors to teach from time to time, to 'maintain their links with the profession'. I partly agree with this, particularly where one special company is involved, like the Bristol Old Vic, or the Royal Shakespeare Company and the Guildhall School of Music and Drama. And of course there are individual actors and directors who are very brilliant teachers – and it would be nice to think that our drama schools could offer these individuals, when they appear, sufficient inducement, both financial and artistic, to remain at the school.

What I think a little dangerous, because it perpetuates and intensifies the eclectic philosophy of 'have-a-bashery', is the employment of *any* available actor or director on an *ad hoc* basis, without proper consultation and without his being familiar with the policy of the school (if any) and with the rest of the training. Such *ad hoc* 'locums' are often very stimulating to the students – many are talented teachers – but the system is no substitute for a sound, integrated training that has room for the *occasional* outsider with special skills, who is particularly sympathetic to such training. Outsiders often make the students very critical of their regular teachers, often rightly, but this can demonstrate the weakness of the training rather than the genuine talent of the outsider.

Money is most of the answer. First, drama schools should be able to attract the best teachers that can be found, and second, they should pay their staff to travel occasionally to observe other training methods. The third essential is the immediate institution of mandatory grants. Teachers learn from students all the time; if they are not getting the cream of the applicants, the training suffers. How often do we hear of a recognised drama school having to take second-choice students, because their first choices have been unable to obtain grants from their local authority, or have obtained grants only on condition they attend drama courses at local establishments? To let our leading schools spend their meagre resources training second- and often third-choice students is surely artistic and economic madness.

I think our recognised drama schools should be few, at most four in London and six in the regions. I think they should carry mandatory grants so that at least we know we are training the people we want *most* in the profession. I think they should be rather heavily subsidised so that they attract the best teachers, and so that the permanent staff can take sabbaticals to study other training, and outside teachers of outstanding gifts, both British and foreign, can be invited to give substantial courses. In this way we stand a chance of achieving really high standards.

I don't believe drama schools should be run for private profit, though in the current economic climate this will be an unpopular view.

Finally, I'll presume to say what I believe drama schools should really be about: of course they should offer an efficient technical training – the basic minimum that I set out to describe; of course they should have teachers really able to help aspiring actors to act *well* – this is more difficult and extremely rare at present, but *possible*. However, above and beyond this, drama schools should be places that can give their students an appreciation of the art of acting as part of all art, part of history, part of man's deepest needs and aspirations – a real artistic philosophy that will carry the graduate actor cheerfully through some of the worst horrors of 'the business'. This sense of 'connecting' – with the past, with Europe and the world, with other arts and artists and with the future can only be transmitted by *remarkable teachers*. We must find them, we must pay them, and we must see that they have the best drama students in Britain to work with.

A Hobby-horse

Could not student singers be trained *with* actors for part of their first-year course? All the professional singers I know say they would have welcomed classes in acting, reading aloud, verse-speaking, movement, dance and wearing of costume during their training, and most say they did not study full-time, and so would have had the opportunity to fit them in. Of course, music students would have to have their basic solo lessons and music theory classes separately, but actors would benefit greatly from most of the choral work. In fact I believe all the students would benefit, whether they eventually became actors, opera singers, concert artists, or even oratorio and *lieder* singers.

A Further Hobby-horse

Standard English

This is now often called Received Pronunciation. I don't really like either term: *whose* standard? received from *whom*?

There is often a resistance in students to acquiring Standard English on the grounds that it sounds posh or snobby. It's important to emphasise certain points.

Standard English is not the same as posh English. Posh English for the actor is a dialect like any other, varies according to character, background, age and period, and should be studied as carefully as any other dialect.

Nobody (I hope) expects an actor to alter his native speech in private life unless he wants to. (Though perhaps in public, for instance in media interviews, as guardians of the language we work in, it's a good idea for actors to use 'correct' grammar and vocabulary. Perhaps not?)

But I do wish that we had, as the French do, a standard pronunciation that indicates not class but a *concern* for the language – a robust, flexible, serviceable speech, carrying no special social or regional connotations, but useful for work in, for example, translated plays (where neither Sloane nor any broad regional dialect would be appropriate) – or in period texts, where if we spoke as the characters of the time actually did speak, we should frequently be incomprehensible to a modern audience. It's hard to find the right term: 'Actors' English' suggests the Edwardian throb of an actor-laddie; 'Educated English' carries overtones of academicism. Yet surely no actor should feel *ashamed* of being educated. There ought to be a form of speech that reflects education and culture without sounding prissy or academic or exclusive in any way. In practice, most of our successful actors and actresses do aim for and achieve such a speech, whatever their background. Why are students scared of it?

Yet Another Hobby-Horse

Phrasing

This seems no longer to be taught in drama schools. Drama graduates are less and less able to handle classical texts with skill, wit and almost as important, with rapidity. A good ear and reasonable facility with text is invaluable to the actor, and most of our successful performers in all areas have it. But it is not taught in the schools. I run a workshop at the Actors' Centre called 'How to Get the Laughs with the Words', crudely subtitled by me, 'If You Can Phrase Properly You Will Earn More Money'. It is always packed.

PART IV

Conference of Drama Schools

The Arts Educational London Schools

Cone Ripman House, 14 Bath Road, London W4 1LY,
Tel: 0181-994 9366

Courses offered:

A formal academic and vocational training for pupils between
8 and 16 years.
3-year Dance Course + 2 A Levels
3-year Musical Theatre Course + 2 A Levels
3-year Adult Drama Course
2-year A Level Foundation Drama Course
1-year Postgraduate Acting Company

The Schools in London and Tring, Hertfordshire, have a celebrated history over the past seventy years, with a long list of
distinguished alumni. In new premises again, all courses continue
to thrive and the main drama course includes a new Postgraduate
Course/Acting Company which will provide a useful development for mature students or professional actors. It is a chance to
refocus previous work in the environment of a professional
theatre company and seeks to offer a fully realistic daily training
to augment production work.

The Drama Course now operates from the London address.

Pupils who attend the day or boarding school, where they
combine academic secondary education with dance, drama or
music, will still have to audition for the adult courses along with
outside applicants once they have reached the required minimum
age.

Birmingham School of Speech and Drama

45 Church Road, Birmingham B15 3SW, Tel: 0121-454 3424

Founded in 1936 and now set in pleasant grounds near the city centre the school offers:

3-year Acting Course – NCDT approved
2-year Stage Management Course
1-year Postgraduate Course
2-year Teaching Course

The experience of the staff and outline in the prospectus appear very strongly focused on speech and poetry.

The audition adds the requirement of a lyrical poem and a song, plus sight-reading, improvisation and movement. The 2-year Teaching Course is linked to the requirements of the Speech and Drama Training Diplomas such as Guildhall and LAMDA.

Birmingham like Bristol is an ideal alternative centre to London for training with major television companies and theatres in the city centre. Other large regional companies close by include Coventry (Belgrade) and Stratford (Royal Shakespeare Company).

Bristol Old Vic Theatre School

1 Downside Road, Clifton, Bristol BS8 2XF, Tel: 01272-733535

Founded in 1946 by Laurence Olivier alongside the Bristol Old Vic Company, it continues a close association with the Theatre Royal and the West Country in general.
Courses offered:

3-year Acting Course
2-year Acting Course
1-year Postgraduate Vocational Attachment
2-year HND Performing Arts–Stage Management
1-year Wardrobe Course
Trainee Director's Attachment
1-year Design Course

Auditionees have always spoken highly of the Weekend Schools, which last from 6.45 p.m. on a Friday to 3.45 p.m. on a Saturday and give students a chance to feel the atmosphere of the town and school, and work with most members of the staff. These weekends are for a selected few invited from the preliminary auditions, from which final selection is made. The school offers five performing venues in and around its own premises, plus a host of touring venues in the region. The school's philosophy is to avoid 'tags and labels' as Chekhov says and the training is very much run as a professional theatre company with a strong classical background.

It is an ideal contrast to the London-dominated schools, being away from such a stressed metropolis yet within easy reach of excellent theatres in Bristol and nearby Bath, Exeter, Worcester and Stratford. The BBC operates its West Country studios from Bristol.

Rose Bruford College of Speech and Drama

Lamorbey Park, Sidcup, Kent DA15 9DF, Tel: 0181-300 3024

School of Theatre
3-year BA Hons Acting; Actor-Musician; Theatre Writing

School of Production
3-year BA Hons Lighting Design; Stage Management; Costume Design and Wardrobe; Scenic Construction and Properties; Theatre Design; Music Technology

All courses are validated by the University of Kent, Canterbury.

The college now has two sites – the new space at Greenwich offers rehearsal, television and radio studios as well as seminar and lecture rooms. Future plans at Lamorbey Park include a new theatre, library and studio accommodation.

The present courses offered have developed substantially from the original founded by Miss Bruford in the 1950s. The setting is ideal and spacious including a country house, a lake and extensive grounds, an old barn theatre, workshops, wardrobe and an excellent library. Major productions are performed in London theatres for maximum exposure to agents and casting directors, though the College itself is within easy reach of London's West End and close to the Churchill Theatre, Bromley, and the Greenwich Theatre.

Central School of Speech and Drama

Embassy Theatre, 64 Eton Avenue, London NW3 3HY, Tel: 0171-722 8183

Alongside LAMDA, RADA and Webber-Douglas this school has a long and distinguished history dating back to its inception in 1906 by the legendary Elsie Fogerty and Sir Frank Benson. Since the days when it nurtured the great talents of Lord Olivier,

Dame Peggy Ashcroft and Dame Judi Dench it has changed and enlarged dramatically. In 1972 the school became grant-aided by the then ILEA and collaborated with various polytechnics for its fine and respected courses in Speech Therapy and Speech and Drama Teacher Training. Many students may feel drawn to careers in teaching drama, or specialising in Advanced Drama Therapy for people with any kind of disability or mental illness. The general prospectus details these courses as well as those offering a professional theatre training. There cannot be a better environment to learn in while being able to draw on so much practical performance.

The Stage Department offers the following:

3-year Acting Course
2-year Stage Management Course

There is no stated philosophy though the word 'Central' was chosen originally to avoid extremism.

Cygnet Theatre Company

Cygnet Training Theatre, Friars Gate, Exeter, Devon EX2 4AZ, Tel: 01392-77189

The School is situated in a secluded, residential part of the city, near the river and within easy reach of the city centre. There is an on-going link between the Northcott Theatre, Exeter and the Theatre Royal, Plymouth. Former trainees have worked in both theatres, as well as with the Orchard Theatre, the local touring company for the South West.

Cygnet accepts flexible young actors with a mature attitude who are expected to work with a fully professional commitment from their first day. High standards of technique and flexibility are aimed for, and, among others, the disciplines of Stanislavsky, Michael Chekov and Michel Saint-Denis are in constant use. Cygnet has a good professional standing as a touring company, and aims to provide maximum contacts and work opportunities for its leaving actors. The ethic on which the company's work is based is strongly influenced by Peter Brook. Because Cygnet's method of training in a working theatre environment is unique, it is not a conventional drama school. Cygnet actors have an exceptionally high success rate in obtaining professional work as a result of appearances and contacts made during touring and of the professional polish that so much experience of public performances gives them. This should encourage local education authorities to give financial help to applicants who obtain places, of which there are only eight each year.

Founded in 1980, the Company grew out of an association between Monica Shallis, Mary Evans and the Northcott Theatre, then under the direction of Richard Digby Day. Cygnet is now a full-time training company, which functions like a small-scale touring company, drawing its members from all over the UK and abroad. Applicants must be 18 or over. No specific academic qualifications are required. Professional actors may join the Company for three to six months to refresh skills or study and tour in a specific role.

Formal training in voice, movement, music, dance, etc., are all part of the daily work of the Company, but rehearsal and performance remain the strongest features of the experience-based training. The year is divided into three terms of twelve weeks, with classwork each morning and rehearsal each afternoon for ten weeks, and touring in the South West for the last two weeks. In the summer term there is more extensive touring, often with open-air performances, and the Company usually takes one or two productions to the Edinburgh Festival.

Normally the course runs over nine terms starting in September; entry is possible in January in special circumstances. *Additional options*: Acting with Music, Acting with Directing, Acting with Stage Management. Applicants must be 18 years and over. No specific academic qualifications are required.

Drama Centre London

176 Prince of Wales Road, London NW5 3PT, Tel: 0171-267 1177

Since breaking away from the Central School twenty-nine years ago, the staff who formed the Drama Centre have created and maintained a positive and systematic approach to training actors. It is simply an approach that actors fit into rather than one that they create themselves. Therefore it is a tough course and many students don't survive but it has proved excellent for many, including Pierce Brosnan, Simon Callow, John Duttine, Colin Firth, Rupert Frazer and Deborah Norton. These and other actors and directors make impressive reading in so short a time. The prospectus is fascinating and clearly describes the experience of studying there and gives a useful introduction to the staff. The Principal in his Foreword urges prospective students to find out in detail about any school before applying.

All students would be advised to read this prospectus in any event as a contrast to all others.

The courses offered are:

3-year Acting Course (intake 30)
2-year Professional Instructor's Course
A weekend foundation course held every weekend during term-time between April and September

The methodological approach as described in the prospectus bases its work on a fusion of Stanislavsky and Rudolf Laban's innovative work in modern dance. It is a very hard school.

In the Foreword to the Drama Centre prospectus, Christopher Fettes says: 'A remarkably high proportion of those who apply for entrance to theatre schools do so without ever asking themselves what they need to learn or what they expect a school to provide; without bothering too greatly to find out what the various schools are like, how they work, or what distinguishes one from another. Yet good, bad or indifferent, a drama school is going to leave its mark on its students for a lifetime.'

East 15 Acting School

Hatfields, Rectory Lane, Loughton, Essex IG10 3RU,
Tel: 0181-508 5983

Sherriff Hutton Hall, Sherriff Hutton, North Yorkshire YO6 1RH,
Tel: 01347-878442

3-year Acting Course
1-year Postgraduate Course
1-year Stage Management Course
Director's and Tutor's Courses

The school was founded in 1961 by Margaret Bury, continuing her work from the famous Theatre Workshop begun by Joan Littlewood. The task of her school is to marry the brilliant improvisation of Joan Littlewood with method and technique based presently on Stanislavsky, Laban, Feldenkrais and Darwin. The period settings and grounds of the schools in Loughton and Yorkshire abound in atmosphere and offer a real environment for creative work, plus the stunning Corbett Theatre, a converted medieval tithe barn, seating 120. There is a wide variety of students enrolled on all the courses which makes for a colourful and enriching training.

Guildford School of Acting

Millmead Terrace, Guildford, Surrey GU2 5AT, Tel: 01483-60701

Guildford offers a variety of training options out of these main courses:

- 3-year Acting Diploma *or*
- 3-year BA Hons Theatre Option (University of Surrey)
- 1-year Acting Course, for mature students or graduates
- 2-year Stage Management Course (1-year option available for mature students)

The student numbers average 200 and classes are taken in full, half- and quarter groups with individual tutorials for singing, voice and Alexander Technique.

Performance spaces consist of: a 98-seat proscenium theatre, an 80–180 adaptable studio theatre, a 50-seat studio and the rented Mill Theatre.

The school occupies five sites (18 studios) in this very pleasant and historic town. Easy access is available to the Yvonne Arnaud Theatre, Guildford, the Redgrave at Farnham and the Thorndike at Leatherhead as well as some involvement with the University of Surrey.

The prospectus is attractive, well laid out and full of detail regarding course content. The accent for the performer is on flexibility so there are three main disciplines, acting, singing and dancing. The acting option particularly mentions character building and mask work as well as mime.

There are no evening classes but a four-week intensive summer course is available July–August, which is a good way to see if you would respond to the atmosphere and environment. Options are the Standard Classical or Modern Text with many overseas students participating in these summer programmes.

For those not keen on big cities training here away from the stress of traffic noise and pollution is a big plus, especially with three good regional theatres so close at hand.

An excellent establishment for the all-round performer with a good permanent and professional staff to see you through.

Guildhall School of Music and Drama

Silk Street, Barbican, London EC2Y 8DT, Tel: 0171-628 2571

Courses offered:

> 3-year AGSM Diploma Course in Acting
> 3-year BA Hons Course in Acting (City University)
> 3-year BA Hons Course in Stage Management and Technical Theatre (City University)
> Private tuition for part-time students in Drama, Speech Training, Spoken English, Public Speaking and Verse Speaking
> Lecture Course for the LGSM Teacher's Diploma Examination in Speech and Drama

The school here is part of Western Europe's largest complex of arts facilities including the School of Music and the London Symphony Orchestra, and the drama course has some links with the Royal Shakespeare Company.

Currently there are about 700 full-time students enrolled, including 75 actors, 44 stage management and four scene painters. There are two theatres in the school, the main one seating a maximum of 380. It is fully equipped and can be arranged for proscenium (with or without orchestra pit), theatre in the round, thrust or traverse productions. The other theatre is a small studio with a maximum capacity of about 80. There is also a well-equipped recording studio (for radio work) and some basic video equipment plus outside projects in television.

The acting core doesn't follow any one avenue exclusively but gives a very detailed approach to character in various ways, according to the particular needs of each group, but always including the marvellous animal workshop of Michel Saint-Denis.

Registrations begin on 1 October each year and only the first 700 are auditioned. With the top schools receiving anything between 1500 and 2000 applicants per year, you'll have to be quick to get a crack at this school if you think you're good enough.

Head of voice here is Patsy Rodenburg who is also head of voice at the Royal National Theatre and is arguably the top vocal coach in the world today.

London Academy of Music and Dramatic Art

226 Cromwell Road, London SW5 0SR, Tel: 0171-373 9883

Founded in 1861, LAMDA has a worldwide reputation through its actor training, examination programme and its famous Fulbright Overseas Course. It also has a fine experimental theatre, the MacOwan, the first of its kind in England. It opened in 1963 with Peter Brook's 'Theatre of Cruelty' season. It also runs its technical course in conjunction with Theatre Projects Ltd, the largest group of companies in the world for technical supplies, consultancy and production.
Courses offered are:

3-year Acting Course
1-year Postgraduate Overseas Course
2-year Stage Management and Technical Theatre Course
4-week Shakespeare Summer Workshop

It seems that a top-class summer course of four weeks is an excellent starting point to gain the feel of a 3-year professional training and find out about other London schools and the theatre scene in general.

Together with many other top schools, LAMDA has a long history of successful students and it would be unfair to list only a few. However, it is exciting to see recent graduates from the past ten years winning top international awards and LAMDA has had a good share of success.

Manchester Metropolitan University

School of Theatre, The Capitol Building, School Lane, Didsbury, Manchester M20 0HT, Tel: 0161-247 2000 ext 7123

3-year Acting Course

The School of Theatre is housed in the Capitol Building at East Didsbury (four miles south of the centre of Manchester), together with the School of Film and Television, which provides a full professional range of facilities for the production and recording of television plays, etc. Consequently there is considerable inter-change of ideas and opportunities for projects involving the students and staff of both schools.

There is an especially close relationship between the School of Theatre and television and theatre companies in the North West, most of whom send representatives to see final-year students' annual auditions held in London and Manchester.

The course is plagued with present cuts and a general under-funding. You will find no glossy brochure here but don't be put off. The typed information is clear and interesting, particularly in the general outline where the course seeks to develop the critical faculties of the performer alongside the main acting core:

(a)   A broad perspective of the wide range of events that may be classed as Theatre;
(b)   To have respect for, and discipline in, the execution of the craft of acting;
(c)   To have confidence in their potential to make a unique contribution to the Theatre, and/or related performance media.

Mountview Theatre School

A Conservatoire For The Performing Arts, 104 Crouch Hill, London N8 9EA, Tel: 0181-340 5885

Mountview, established fifty years ago, has grown over the years into one of the most flourishing drama schools in Britain offering highly successful vocational training courses in the following areas:

3-year Acting and Musical Theatre Course
2-year Stage Management, Technical Theatre and Design Course
1-year Acting and Musical Theatre Course
1-year Directors Course
Summer School and Workshops

All full-time courses are vocational which allows students to develop practical promotional skills as well as undergoing intensive artistic training. The school's curricula are constantly updated to match the ever-changing needs of the profession and this has been borne out by the widespread success of Mountview's graduates in virtually every area of the performing arts.

Mountview also has an international reputation and has over the years toured to Sweden, Russia, America, Italy and Holland. All courses are accredited by the NCDT (National Council For Drama Training) and the organisation is also one of the eighteen members of the CDS (Conference of Drama Schools), a member of ELIA (European League of the Institute of the Arts) and an associate member of URTA (University Resident Theatre Association) in full in the USA. Discretionary awards are available for overseas students and the school is certified by the Department of Health, Education and Welfare, USA, for Guaranteed Federally Insured Students' Loan program.

Queen Margaret College

Clerwood Terrace, Edinburgh EH12 8TS, Tel: 0131-317 3000

4-year BA Hons Acting
4-year BA Hons Drama-Studies
4-year BA Hons Stage Management and Theatre Production
1-year (full or part-time) PG DIP Community Theatre

Founded in 1875, the present buildings, five miles outside Edinburgh city centre, are on a 24-acre site. The drama students have access to the other facilities of the College, which include sporting amenities, study bedrooms, Student Association social events, dining halls and self-catering units. The drama training here has radically altered in the past few years, demanding greater facilities, forging stronger and wider links with the theatre profession both in the UK and abroad.

Royal Academy of Dramatic Art

62–64 Gower Street, London WC1E 6ED, Tel: 0171-636 7076

Founded by Sir Herbert Beerbohm Tree in 1904, RADA stands as the premier school set-up with all the pomp of the British Empire, Edwardian England and the gentleman actor. A rare piece of silent film remains of the inaugural board meeting, chaired by Sir George Alexander of the St James's Theatre, surrounded by most of the knighted actor-managers of London. The strength of that image lingered long into the second half of this century despite changing styles towards more naturalistic performance. The stigma of the RADA voice has finally been buried though the 'Royal' image still attracts some of the most talented in the land. The list of great names and exciting talent is endless though many will still recall the magical few years when a 'golden age' threw up a mine of talent all at once: Peter O'Toole, Sian Phillips, Alan Bates, Tom Courtenay, Albert Finney, Glenda Jackson, *et al.*, all heralding a new style of actor on the West End stage and screen.

In recent years too it has spawned graduates of distinction from the Stage Management Course who have succeeded in far wider fields than the course could ever hope to encompass.

The Courses
   Acting – 3 years (28 students per year)
   Stage Management – 2 years (6 students, 3 times a year)

Specialist Courses
   Scene Design (4 terms)
   Stage Carpentry (4 terms)
   Stage Electrics (4 terms)
   Property Making (4 terms)

Classes
   Regular weekly voice and movement classes are held by the staff for professional actors.

Summer School
   A 4-week summer school is held annually and is a good way of getting the feel of a school and of drama training. Also it provides a chance to see theatre in London with expert guidance and comment available.

The present accommodation has three in-house performance spaces including the 350-seater rebuilt Vanbrugh Theatre. Plans are afoot to expand for film and television and further specialist work in technical areas. This may mean a move to another part of London if suitable premises can be found.

   The audition process lists two provisions which are good general guidelines:
(1)   Only one of the two pieces may be a direct address to the audience such as a speech by Chorus or narrator. This gives you fair warning that you must not avoid 'character' even unwittingly.
(2)   A list of certain speeches which should be avoided at audition will be given. A very wise precaution. So take heed for other schools. After years of several hundred renderings of a set piece the poor audition panel is likely to go blank instantly when you mention the 'ring' speech from *Twelfth Night*. Do give yourselves a chance!

Royal Scottish Academy of Music and Drama

100 Renfrew Street, Glasgow G2 3BD, Tel: 0141-332 4101

The origins of the RSAMD go back as far as 1847, and in the United Kingdom it stands as one of the four Royal Schools of Music and one of the two Royal Academies of Dramatic Art. It moved 100 years later into splendid new purpose-built premises opened by the Queen Mother. With a complement of around 500 students in Music and Drama, plus staff, the building was an enormous undertaking and consists of a concert hall, Georgian theatre, recital room, laboratory theatre, television studio, wardrobe, library, workshop, rehearsal and practice rooms. Like the Guildhall it can offer drama students that special opportunity of mixing with the other disciplines of opera and music plus occasional combined performances.

The School of Drama offers:

3-year Acting Course (possible BA)
3-year BA (Dramatic Studies) Course (Hons)
2-year HND Production and Technical Stage Management
Junior School of Drama (10–16 years)

There is a long-standing relationship with the Jacques Lecoq School (see Mime Courses) where selected graduates undertake a postgraduate work.

Webber-Douglas Academy of Dramatic Art

30 Clareville Street, London SW7 5AP, Tel: 0171-370 4154

In operation for over sixty years, this famous school has provided actors ranging from Michael Denison, Dulcie Gray, Donald Sinden, Angela Lansbury and Stewart Granger to Terence Stamp, Steven Berkoff, Charlotte Cornwell, Anthony Sher, Anita Dobson and Leslie Grantham. Despite its cramped accommodation and large student body of around 120 it has managed to survive in the expensive and densely populated South Kensington area.

Presently the courses offered are:

3-year Diploma Course – Acting
2-year Diploma Course — Acting
1-year Postgraduate Course
5-week Summer Course (60 students maximum)

Being in Central London the school is able to call on a wide variety of experienced staff and directors though no method or fixed approach to acting is stipulated. The Principal speaks of his aim to create a well-rounded actor through the foundation skills of voice, movement and acting technique. The study of Shakespeare and other classical periods is at the core of the course, but as the course progresses the emphasis shifts towards modern works. Other opportunities are available to work as a director and stage manager and there is an emphasis on singing. Directing and stage management are contained within the main courses and not offered as specialisations.

Classes are taught in various local premises but the main building houses the Chanticleer Theatre, seating 100, with nearby a 40-seat studio theatre.

Welsh College of Music and Drama

Castle Grounds, Cathays Park, Cardiff CF1 3ER, Tel: 01222-371440

Inaugurated in 1949, the College has been in its new building since 1973 with a combined music and drama student population of around 350. Like the Guildhall and the Royal Scottish, students here enjoy a free-flow relationship with various disciplines in the arts.

> 3-year BA Theatre Studies with options in acting, design or stage management
> 1-year Advanced Diploma in Drama with options in acting, directing, design or stage management

The training, though universal, has a particular focus towards Welsh theatre with the growing number of local theatre-in-education companies, community theatres, Welsh radio and television offering technical and performance opportunities.

The 3-year Graduate Course offers an extra unit embracing Dramatic Criticism and Theatre Studies leading to a Diploma of the University of Wales as well as the College diploma.

A Selection of Independent Schools

There has been a proliferation of new studio courses over the last few years. The demand on theatre studies has grown with the up-surge in unemployment and the declining interest in the sciences of a nuclear age. Many top schools reflect that though the numbers auditioning have doubled recently, despite the cost of auditioning and course fees, the talent is no greater and it is still hard to find a good balanced, talented group each year. Where do the others all go to? Many of them will get in to the many small studios where they need 'numbers', including 'dead wood', in order to survive. Through financial restrictions many talented actors cannot afford a 3-year day-time course and are forced to opt for a shorter course or even an evening school.

Among these studio courses and even larger establishments the American influence of doctrinaire or methodological training rears its head. Sometimes it can be an honourable attempt to impart a more formalised method than we are used to but in the wrong hands it becomes popularly known in London theatre circles as 'acting by numbers'. The worst excesses of this guru-like teaching are nothing less than brain-washing. In fact in the past few years no fewer than three London students have ended up in psychiatric hospitals. Therefore, beware of courses that profess certain goals in this area – try to see their work first and decide for yourself by talking to current students in order to find out whether the training is indulgent and selfish.

Even talking to those students may be a mistake, as they may be attracted by 'intellectual non-doing' and may love indulging, or they may be rejects of major schools who stand no hope of success within the business today.

You need a stable personality with a good life experience and a realistic approach to survive some of the strong personalities around these areas. Again beware – be street-wise!

There is not enough space to list and discuss many courses but a sample visited will give you a good guide to reputable alternative training.

Drama Studio London

1 Grange Road, London W5 5QN, Tel: 0181-579 3897

Founded in 1966 in London, this school offers a 1-year course only to postgraduates or advanced students. It is a very expensive training, though according to the elegant prospectus, discretionary grants may be available through its NCDT accreditations.
Courses offered:

1-year Acting Course
1-year Directing Course

In January 1995 the school opened its first purpose-built performance space called the Grange Court Theatre.

The London Academy of Performing Arts

2 Effie Road, Fulham Broadway, London SW6 1TB,
Tel: 0171-736 0121 Fax: 0171-371 5624

2-year Diploma in Acting Course
2-year Musical Theatre Option
1-year Graduate Acting Course
1-year Director's Course
1-year Stage Management Course
Summer Shakespearean Acting Courses (Beginners/ Advanced)
12-week Classical Acting Course

An established centrally based Drama School with integral theatre facilities, lecture and practice rooms. A recognised part of the programme is usage of fully equipped television and broadcasting studios as well as established theatres and schools in London and the local borough of Hammersmith and Fulham – including the Lyric Theatre.

The Academy has a distinguished resident staff and maintains the policy of inviting talented working directors to direct the Academy's productions. Experience tells that the courses lead to a high level of employment once Diploma and Postgraduate actors leave; both groups regularly achieving a wide recognition in all major areas of dramatic arts both at home and abroad.

The London Studio Centre

42–50 York Way, London N1 9AB, Tel: 0171-837 7741

3-year Performing Arts Course

Founded in 1978 by the distinguished dancer and choreographer, Bridget Espinosa, this well-equipped school has developed an overall course that specialises in dance, drama, music, singing, film and television technique. It provides a bridge between school leaving and entry into the professional theatre, aiming at the 16–23-year-olds. Other courses exist for specialist work in advance ballet and music.

With the rise in status worldwide of the British musical, far greater demands are being made on artists in this country. At the time of writing there are fifteen London musicals playing, some for long periods, needing a large turnover in replacement casts. A more comprehensive training such as this does enable the dancer–singer–actor to be more accomplished in all three areas and to move from musicals to drama in theatre, television and film. The facilities and staff here are excellent and over 500 classes per week are available to the 350 students who attend per year. Timetables are specially designed for each individual to take account of their varying levels in the different subjects.

The course is accredited by the Council for Dance Education.

Oxford School of Drama

Sansomes Farm Studios, Woodstock, Oxford OX7 1ER, Tel. 01993-812883

A very smart, intelligent and inviting prospectus heralds the various courses that have been growing here over the past fifteen years. A distinguished staff of working professional directors boosts the permanent staff who teach a small number of students in a glorious country setting on the Blenheim Palace estate. The proximity to Oxford provides an excellent historic setting for research and atmosphere. The school can also arrange supervised accommodation in Oxford for students.

2-year Acting Course
1-year Postgraduate Acting Course
4-term Stage Management Course
The Edinburgh Festival Performance Course – 4 weeks
Introduction to Acting Courses – 2 weeks (summer)
Advanced Acting Courses – 2 weeks (summer)

The 4-week Edinburgh Festival Performance Course is a unique idea and consists of improvisations and workshops in part of the first week leading to rehearsal of specially commissioned pieces. The basic fees include the full cost of staging the production, transport to and from Edinburgh/Oxford, self-catering accommodation in Edinburgh and membership of the Festival Fringe Society and Fringe Club.

The full-time course description presents a well-explained summary of structure – a lesson to some other schools in terms of lay-out and clearly stated rationale. The training is strongly drawn from the work of Michel Saint-Denis and Uta Hagen and is intimate enough to give first-class attention and opportunities.

Richmond Drama School

Richmond Adult and Community College, Parkshot, Richmond, Surrey TW9 2RE, Tel: 0181-940 0170

1-year Acting Course

In pleasant surroundings opposite Richmond station and just around the corner from the Orange Tree theatre is the Richmond College, called the Parkshot Centre. Picking up the remnants of the old Q Theatre and subsequent De Leon Drama School is a 1-year programme in acting with 22 students currently enrolled. The atmosphere and staff are friendly and welcoming and are housed in a separate building from the main college, which it shares with other performing arts disciplines. It is a compact set-up with limited funding from its own fees but with overheads underwritten by the main college. So far it is managing to dip into most areas of work that can be covered in one year and has established links to enable further facilities including a gymnasium.

The Adult College is a thriving environment with a small theatre, two excellent rehearsal/classrooms, plus access to an attractive café and exhibition area. Some authorities will fund students even though it cannot be accredited. However, fees for private students are very low – in fact a quarter of, say, the Drama Studio course.

Strong links have been forged with the thriving Orange Tree theatre plus the school offers a nationally recognised diploma. Validated by the University of Oxford and Surrey and South West London Access Agency, this is especially helpful for those wishing to gain access to higher education.

The Poor School And Workshop Theatre

242 Pentonville Road, London N1 9JY, Tel: 0171-837 6030

2-year Acting Course

This school was created in 1986 in response to the need for a first-class training which was financially within the reach of most students. The training is divided into six terms though all classes take place in the evenings and weekends until the final two terms when daytime work is involved. Twenty-eight students are accepted each October.

After recent fund-raising the school has opened a studio theatre, the Workhouse, seating between 50 to 80. There is a large committed staff of experienced teachers including the illustrious George Hall, who was head of the acting course at Central School for twenty-three years.

Other Courses

The Actors' Institute

137 Goswell Road, London EC1V 7ET, Tel: 0171-251 8178

The Actors' Institute was founded in New York in 1977 by its creative director Dan Fauci who conceived and developed the Mastery, Samurai, Creativity and Leadership courses and the coaching programme. It provides an environment where creative people can come to risk, experiment, learn and share skills and generate their own work. Its purpose is to create a spirit of excitement and inspiration, to facilitate new ideas and to support people in making a creative impact in whatever career they have chosen.

As well as offering classes and workshops, the Institute provides a place for people to meet and generate projects. Members of the Institute have been instrumental in forming co-operative agencies and a number of theatrical, film and video projects. Courses are open to all ages and appeal to mature persons who want to make a break from present work to see if they have what it takes to act. Apart from the acting classes for all levels, there are sessions in song-writing, audition technique, stand-up, Alexander Technique and voice-over work.

The Central London Adult Education Institute

West End Area, The City Literary Institute, Stukeley Street, Drury Lane, London WC2B 5LJ, Tel: 0171-242 9872

Known affectionately as the 'City Lit' over many years, this mainly evening institute has a thriving Drama, Dance and Speech department run by the indefatigable John James. Courses vary from movement, voice, acting through to acrobatics, masks, mime, and clown workshops. In all there are more than 120 separate courses — ranging from one-day to a two-year part-time acting training. The great advantage here is the wide range of choice plus the incredibly low fees charged. It makes for a very attractive beginning to and preparation for any full-time training, as a refresher or as a means of developing certain specialisations. You are advised to book early for these courses as the demand is heavy with a waiting list of around three thousand.

Information can be obtained on 0171-430 0544.

Morley College Theatre School

61 Westminster Bridge Road, London SE1 7HT, Tel: 0171-928 8501

As well as a general education programme there are a few evening and Saturday morning drama sessions including a Youth Theatre Group. Courses tend to be in two-term blocks and students are expected to attend every session. The music and opera groups have achieved a well-deserved reputation for their constant high standard of performance.

Mountview Arts Centre

Ralph Richardson Memorial Studios, 1 Kingfisher Place, Clarendon Road, London N22 6NY, Tel: 0181-889 8110

In large premises, the part-time courses have expanded over the last forty years and consist of:

Foundation Acting Course
　1-year 3 evenings per week over 33 weeks divided into three terms, hours: 7–10 p.m.
　This is useful if you are considering a full 3-year course eventually.

Evening Acting Course
　1 or 2 years for interested and keen amateurs.

Teenage Courses
　Acting and Dance Courses available for 12–17-year-olds, one evening per week from 6 to 8 p.m.

Children's Courses
　Acting, Dance and Graded Modern Dance for 6–12-year-olds. Classes are usually held on Friday evenings (early) and Saturdays.

Other courses include:
  Jazz and Tap Classes
  Writers' Forum
  Piano Classes
  Keep Fit
  Mountview Choir
  Children's Choir
  Easter and Summer Workshops for 8–14-year-olds, 1-week
    duration.

Drama Degrees

Note: University drama courses are not included in this book, which covers full-time practical training only.

Bretton Hall College of Higher Education

West Bretton, Wakefield, West Yorkshire WF4 4LG, Tel: 01924-830261

> 3-year BA Hons Theatre Arts or Dramatic Arts
> 2-year MA Contemporary Performing Art

This latter course is unique and offers a programme to suit teachers, tutors, theatre practitioners, youth leaders and community workers who want to develop their expertise in theatrical work and extend their range of understanding and practice.

The first degree is validated and awarded by the University of Leeds and there is an arrangement for students to attend a summer school at New York University.

Dartington College of Arts

Totnes, Devon TQ9 6EJ, Tel: 01803-862224

> 3-year BA Hons Theatre
> 3-year BA Hons Performance Writing

The course aims through training and exploration in movement, directing, writing and performance to engage people in the activity of theatre-making. It is for people who wish to place themselves and their resources in those communities the established theatre has not served. Nearby in Totnes is a Centre for Alexander Training which is associated with the College and benefits all students.

Mime Courses

Desmond Jones School of Mime

20 Thornton Avenue, London W4 1QG, Tel: 0181-747 3537

3-month courses annually

This school is the longest-established school of mime in Britain. Its international reputation encompasses students from more than forty countries.

The course is a fusion of two main approaches: teaching physical technique to a high level of expertise, and mime acting, where pupils are encouraged and guided into exploring their own creativity and personality, and expanding their ways of playing. The courses lasts three months and includes work on classical and modern mime, illusion and abstract techniques, characterisation and caricature, story-telling, vocal and verbal improvisation, masks, walking, *commedia dell'arte*, movement analysis and body language – all in varying degrees of stylisation.

The mime technique is based on that of Etienne Decroux, the originator of the modern mime. The acting technique draws on a variety of sources from Jacques Lecoq to Keith Johnstone. This school can be seen as a stimulating prelude to the more conventional study of speaking theatre.

Ecole Jacques Lecoq

57 rue du Faubourg Saint-Denis, 75010 Paris, France, Tel: (1) 47 70 44 78

For those who would like to specialise after a 2- and 3-year drama training and take a postgraduate 2-year course in mime, where better to go than Paris and the Jacques Lecoq School, founded in 1956. A basic knowledge of French is essential and a stay would bring a golden opportunity to become fluent. With European

Union changes affecting our daily lives and the opening of the Channel Tunnel, barriers are breaking down physically if not temperamentally between Britain and the Continent. There is no entrance examination required, only a detailed CV and photograph. The first term acts as a probationary period with a tough exam for entrance into the second year — only a third of the students survive. There is a special third year for a selected few.

An evening course exists for students obliged to work during the day.

The accommodation is spacious with facilities for video, acrobatic equipment, etc., plus five public shows per year. In recent years 150 British students have studied here, among others from 25 countries. What a marvellous chance to transcend national barriers of language, creed and culture. Britain's most successful export was Steven Berkoff who studied there after training at Webber-Douglas.

Several exciting companies have been formed by ex-students, including Footsbarn and the Moving Picture Mime Show.

A good way to start is to read *Théâtre du geste – mime et acteurs* by Jacques Lecoq (published by Bordas and available through the school).

Those students lucky enough to be taught by ex-students of Lecoq will benefit for ever from the study of animals, neutral masks, character masks, *commedia dell'arte* and clowns to understand the complete mental, physical and vocal language of character.

Stage Schools

Stage schools offer vocational training in conjunction with general education from as early as 5 years.

Four examples are:

Arts Educational London Schools

Cone Ripman House, 14 Bath Road, London W4 1LY,
Tel: 0181-994 9366

The main vocational boarding school is housed in the Rothschild Mansion in Tring Park, Hertfordshire, and along with the London school offers a balanced curriculum in academic and vocational disciplines between the ages of 10 and 16 years of age.

Senior Courses
  3-year Dance Course, 16+ years
  3-year Musical Theatre Course, 16+ years
  2-year Creative Arts A level Course, 16–18 years

The senior drama courses are listed in the first section of this directory.

Barbara Speake Stage School

East Acton Lane, London W3 7EG, Tel: 0181-743 6096

Established in 1945, the school gives a full academic training from 5–17 years.

An agency runs alongside the school for employment in television, films, modelling and stage work.

Italia Conti Academy of Theatre Arts

23 Goswell Road, London EC1M 7AJ, Tel: 0171-608 0047

Junior Course, 9–16 years
3-year Performing Arts Course, 16+ years
1-year Drama Course, 16+ years
Part-time Saturday classes, 3½–18 years, for acting, singing,
ballet, tap and modern dance

Redroofs Theatre School

Day School Department, Harlequin House, 26 Bath Road,
Maidenhead, Berks. Tel: 01628-822982

Student Department, Littlewick Green, Maidenhead, Berks.
SL6 3QY, Tel: 01628 822982

Day School
7–16 years

Student Department
2-year Drama Course 16+ years
1-year Postgraduate Course

Private Coaching

For those who are seeking personal tuition in voice, speech, singing, etc., there is a long list of coaches advertising in each edition of *Contacts*. This publication is a must for all would-be professionals. If you're not sure who to go to, then the *Spotlight* office, who publish *Contacts*, will be only too happy to advise. The Training Department of the Arts Council also keeps lists from time to time of recommended coaches. All these addresses and telephone numbers are in Appendix IV. Standards vary from first class to the horrific 'elocution' teacher, so tread warily. Prices vary too, so do check with friends, teachers, career advisers, etc. For singing it is very hard to find the right teacher for your voice, particularly if acting is your main interest. Try a few until you find one whose imagery you understand. Opinions may vary wildly between them – some may slot you as a mezzo or light baritone, instead of a soprano or tenor. Don't be too gullible – find out as much as you can for yourself and don't be too easily led.

Examination Boards

The following examination boards are established centres for raising standards in speech, drama and communication skills. They are not limited in any way to people wanting to study acting as a future career and indeed they do not necessarily help the potential success of an individual to achieve that goal. However, for the right people they are extremely valuable and give worthwhile exposure to presentation, performance, concentration, speech disciplines and general personality growth and confidence to future actors. Full syllabus and material can be obtained from the following addresses:

The English Speaking Board

26A Princes Street, Southport, Merseyside PR8 1EQ,
Tel: 01704-501730

Founded in 1953 by the renowned Christabel Burniston MBE, although not strictly theatre-orientated, the ESB provides an invaluable service in improving standards of oral communication in most walks of life for students in further and higher education, or those training for commercial, technical, industrial or professional occupations. The ESB courses can be useful for anyone wishing to improve their speaking voice, telephone voice or confidence in handling staff.

The Guildhall School of Music and Drama

Barbican, London EC2Y 8DT, Tel: 0171-628 2571

The Guildhall runs a similar syllabus of examinations to that of the London Academy (see below) and successful candidates may reach the highest teaching award of LGSM to use after their names.

The London Academy of Music and Dramatic Art

Examinations Department, 226 Cromwell Road, London SW5 0SR, Tel: 0171-373 4337

Grade exams include Speaking of Verse and Prose, Song Recital, Reading, Spoken Engish, Public Speaking, Choral Speaking, Acting and Mime. The two highest acting awards give successful candidates ALAM and LLAM after their names. These are recognised and respected credentials for those seeking teaching of speech and drama posts privately, or within a formal educational establishment.

London College of Music

47 Great Marlborough Street, London W1V 2AS, Tel: 0171-437 6120

Again dating back over a hundred years, from 1887, the LCM offers Speech and Drama examinations in grades up to teacher status, including Oral Communication and Public Speaking. The highest awards offer the letters FLCM, ALCM, LLCM to add to your name and carry considerable weight in this area of teaching, though, like the other schools listed here, they are not recognised by the Department of Education. Recognition applies only to full-time internal courses.

Trinity School of Music, London

External Examinations Department, 11–13 Mandeville Place, London W1M 6AQ, Tel: 0171-935 5773

Trinity was the first college to devise the system of offering external candidates progressive examinations based on carefully graded syllabuses. Initially these were in music, more than a hundred years ago, and now include Speech and Drama, Effective Speaking, Group Drama, Choral Speech and English as a Foreign Language for students and teachers. These are held in over a thousand centres covering forty countries, with trained examiners sent out from London. The diploma exams lead to the awards of ATCL Associate, LTCL Licentiate, and FTCL Fellow, entitling the holder to an academic gown and hood.

Australian and New Zealand Drama Training

Professional government funded drama training is a very recent development beginning with NIDA in Sydney circa 1958. Its origins and early staffing involved a strong British and European influence. Today there is a far greater local and American flavour to much of the teaching and performance work. New Zealand integrates a strong Maori culture into its work whereas Australia has been slow to find a satisfactory harmony. There are several initiatives now to 'tack on' Aboriginal culture in order to be politically correct. However all the text books that inform the leading establishments are either British, European or American.

The advantage in a late start has meant that there are no infrastructure problems to contend with alongside veteran philosophies and styles pre *Look Back in Anger*. The buildings are new and purpose-built, the staff are young and vigorous, the teaching methods fresh and well constructed. Strong course outlines are required by government with efficient student and staff assessments.

It is not all golden however. There are funding problems in Victoria at the time of going to press – and there will always be staff and student personality problems until there is enough wise counsel to advise and recognise the worthy amongst a thrusting creative society.

The past twelve years have been an exciting challenge for me moving from LAMDA in London to the remotest city in the world – Perth, Western Australia. There has never been a question of talent amongst the students only a cause for concern amongst the academic hierarchy who cannot judge integrity and confuse change with novelty.

The National Institute of Dramatic Art (NIDA)

PO Box 1, Kensington, Sydney, New South Wales 2033, Australia, Tel: 02-697 7607

NIDA is the Australian National Theatre School funded by the federal government through the Department of Communications and the Arts. An independent school located in Sydney, New South Wales, NIDA was established in 1958 and offered the first full-time training for the theatrical profession in Australia. Since then NIDA has maintained a close association with its founding sponsors, the University of NSW and the Australian national broadcaster, the ABC.

Facilities at present comprise four theatres, six rehearsal rooms, specialised teaching studios for technical production, music, sound and computer-aided design, workshops for the manufacturer of scenery, properties and costumes, a library and administrative offices. The building generates an atmosphere of informality with the various work spaces divided by gardens designed to provide an environment for creative work. There are currently plans to build a multi-purpose venue, and to improve the facilities for film and television training.

NIDA enjoys a national and international reputation, and the students are taught by and/or have access to the most distinguished and influential film, theatre and television practitioners in Australia. NIDA graduates are held in high esteem by the arts entertainment industry and their work spans theatre, film and television both in Australia and overseas. High profile NIDA graduates include Pamela Stephenson, Judy Davis, Mel Gibson, Penny Downie, Michael Siberry, Gale Edwards, Jim Sharman, Baz Luhrman and Hugo Weaving.

The Full-Time Courses

NIDA offers the following full-time courses:

- 3-year Bachelor of Dramatic Art in Acting, Design and Technical Production
- 2-year Associate Diploma of Dramatic Art in Theatre Crafts
- 1-year Graduate Diploma of Dramatic Art in Directing
- 1-year Graduate Diploma of Dramatic Art in Movement Studies
- 1-year Graduate Diploma of Dramatic Art in Voice Studies
- 1-year Graduate Diploma of Dramatic Art in Production Management

All courses are accredited, professionally effective and recognised by industry. Entry to NIDA is extremely competitive with applications numbering, on average, 2000 per year.

Once the new facilities are available, consideration will be given to the introduction of new full-time courses in Opera, Music Theatre, Lighting Design, Sound Design and a special postgraduate course for overseas students.

NIDA Company
Established in 1990, the NIDA Company provides research and development opportunities for professional actors, playwrights, directors, composers and designers. These opportunities are realised through the rehearsal and performance of new Australian plays, music-theatre and innovative work, the rehearsal and performance of workshops and play readings, master classes and commissions of new plays.

An equally important aim of the NIDA Company is to establish an association between the school and the profession, and between students and practitioners. The NIDA Company insists students adopt a realistic and contemporary attitude to the work and provides them with valuable training activities working alongside mentors, teachers and role-models. Full-time students participate in NIDA Company productions as actors, stage managers, designers and front-of-house staff.

The Open Program
Established in 1990, the Open Program provides the community access to drama training, in particular school students and teachers who study or teach drama, and who wish to gain practical skills in acting, design, directing and playwriting. Since that time, the NIDA Open Program has expanded rapidly. In 1993, over 5500 people attended Open Program courses and over 100 guests lecturers were engaged to teach a wide variety of drama-related courses.

Other Activities
The Playwrights Studio is a one-year, part-time, non-accredited course. Full-time students participate in selected classes and seminars and regularly give rehearsed readings of new scripts.

The Play Development Program invites a small number of playwrights to develop plays on commission. They are assisted by staff-directed workshops in which full-time students participate.

Aboriginal and Torres Strait Islander Participation. NIDA is seeking to encourage Aboriginal and Torres Strait Islander participation in all sections of the school.

International Exchanges take place with theatre companies and performing arts educational institutions. Staff exchanges have occurred between the Comédie-Française in Paris, the Shanghai Theatre Academy and the National School of Drama, New Delhi.

NIDA seeks to encourage international students to enrol in the postgraduate courses, either as full-time students, or for shorter periods of time through the Study Abroad scheme. NIDA is also undertaking a range of activities with schools and theatres in India, China, Indonesia, South Korea, Hong Kong, Singapore, Taiwan, Malaysia, Thailand and Tonga.

Theatre Training in Australia Conference was initiated by NIDA in 1992. The aim of the inaugural Conference was to bring together theatre practitioners, trainers and educators from Australia and New Zealand to exchange information, discuss projects of mutual interest and to debate current and future developments in Australian society, theatre and theatre training. The Conference has since become an annual event.

Acappella Group and Choir. Two musical initiatives were introduced in 1993 in order to heighten the musical life of NIDA. The NIDACAPPELLA group consists of selected students from all years and courses and is primarily concerned with performance. The NIDA Choir consists of both students and staff and is primarily concerned with the enjoyment of music.

Educational Philosophy of NIDA

NIDA is unique. It is an arts organisation and an educational institution, a technical school and an artistic academy. Central to the artistic and educational philosophy of NIDA is the concept of a practical theatre school: a dramatic conservatorium offering training based on professional practice.

Conservatory training demands that students develop a range of vocational skills closely linked to a body of specialised knowledge: in other words, a practical and theoretical understanding of the nature, principles and history of theatre. This is imparted to students through a carefully structured sequence of interrelated activities during intensive years of study.

The profession of drama is the basic educational practice of the school. This process involves the close collaboration of a team of actors, designers, technical production and craft specialists who are supported and guided by a director and work in association with management. This is the work of a production company, and the structure of NIDA is based on this model.

Those responsible for creating, design, technical production, theatre crafts and manufacture of play productions are students in the process of learning a craft. Those responsible for directing and teaching are members of staff and practising professionals. The Director of NIDA functions as the Artistic Director, and the Administrator as the General Manager, of an artistic organisation.

Directing, design, theatre crafts, production management, voice and movement training, especially offered at the one institution, is unusual.

The Victorian College of The Arts (VCA)

234 St Kilda Road, Melbourne, Victoria 3004, Australia, Tel: 03 685 9300

The Victorian College of The Arts is an affiliated College of the University of Melbourne and occupies a special position within higher education in Australia. It is unique in that it combines within one institution Schools dedicated to training artists in Drama, Dance, Music, Visual Art and Film and Television.

The School of Drama

The School of Drama was established in 1975; staff are drawn from the profession and there is great emphasis placed on teachers being practitioners in their field. The School also uses the services of many guests directors and teachers.

Graduates have entered the profession at all levels, as performers and as technicians, managers, producers, directors, writers and arts officers in the capital cities and in the regions. Many past students have been distinguished by their ability to create their own work opportunities through self and group-devised work, and a number of established theatre groups owe their existence to the early co-operative efforts of graduates.

Approximately 40 students are accepted annually into the 3-year full-time Degree course. The School offers three streams: Acting; Theatre Making for Animateurs, Director and Writers, and Production.

Acting

The Acting stream offers students specialised training in preparation for entry into the profession in theatre, film, television and radio. The craft of the actor demands skill to perform in the classical repertoire and in contemporary and experimental works, as well as the ability to create new work. The actor must, therefore, achieve a high level of versatility that is expressed and explored physically, vocally, imaginatively, emotionally and psychologically.

The acting stream develops that versatility of craft through a combination of skills classes in acting movement and voice and through rehearsal and performance exercises. The training focuses on exploration, finding of form, and performance as part of an on-going process. But skills alone will not allow the artist to grow. The development of an artist is an individual process and that process is allowed and encouraged within the training of the actor at the School of Drama.

Theatre Making for Animateurs, Directors, Writers

The areas of animateuring, directing and writing all share common subjects and are offered within the stream of theatre making. The intention of this grouping is to meet the demands of contemporary theatre by training students with skills in more than one discipline. A number of sessions, particularly in the first year, are held together with acting students and (as well as this) there are joint workshops and classes involving students from all streams. Within the course there are set core subjects but the student can choose to explore certain areas of study in greater detail.

In addition, a concern of the theatre making stream is to place the craft-specific skills acquired by students within a wider artistic, social, cultural and political context.

Animateuring

The aim of this area of the course is to train creative theatre workers who are capable of initiation and realisation of new work, can support others in the developments of bold relevant theatre ventures, and know how to survive financially and administratively in the industry.

The content of the course ranges from classes where the student is presented with models of a variety of non-mainstream theatre (e.g. community theatre, performance art) to practical workshops which present the student with problem-solving tasks in order to gain experience in these areas. Throughout the course, a great deal of emphasis is placed on the acquisition of skills in administration, budgeting, communication, marketing and sourcing of support funding.

Directing

The primary focus of training in the area of directing is upon working with actors in theatre. Directing students are encouraged to develop a personal 'voice' and style as director and are supported in this through a series of skills workshops and tutorials. These cover areas such as approach to text, *mise en scène*, stagecraft, design and production skills, interpretation, workshop exercises, rehearsal process, group-devised works, film and TV, as well as funding and marketing procedures.

There are opportunities to work on practical projects both within and outside the School of Drama.

Writing

Students develop skills in writing primarily for the theatre in a variety of forms. The work focuses on students evolving a sense of personal style and vision. Classes cover such areas as observation and reportage of real-life experience, fictionalisation, models of dramatic structure, word and image, the question of 'character', and writing for radio, film, and television. Through work with fellow students on a range of projects, playwriting skills are developed alongside and out of practical knowledge of the process of theatre.

During the course, students are required to complete specific writing tasks and some of this work may receive workshopping and/or production within the School of Drama.

Production

The production stream is a professionally oriented vocational programme for those intending to work in a range of technical support areas in theatre. The course is practically based and emphasises an understanding of contemporary theatre and the creative processes involved.

The Western Australian Academy of Performing Arts (WAAPA)

Edith Cowan University, 2 Bradford Street, Mount Lawley, Western Australia 6050, Tel: 09-370 6443

The Western Australian Academy of Performing Arts (WAAPA), situated in Perth, is one of the three major theatre training schools in Australia. It was established in 1980 and is the most comprehensive arts training school in Australia. It offers courses in acting, musical theatre, dance, broadcasting, stage management, theatre design, set construction, costume construction, lighting and sound design, and arts management.

The Western Australian Conservatorium of Music and the Western Australian School of Visual Arts are also part of WAAPA where courses in classical music, jazz and contemporary music, painting, ceramics, printmaking, textiles and art therapy are available at Certificate, Advanced Certificate, Bachelors Degree and Masters Degree level.

Courses available are:

- 1-year full-time Certificate of Musical Theatre
- 2-year full-time Advanced Certificate in Aboriginal Music Theatre
- 3-year full-time Diploma of Performing Arts (Theatre)
- 3-year full-time Diploma of Performing Arts (Production & Design)
- 2-year full-time Associate Degree (Broadcasting)
- 3-year full-time Bachelor of Arts (Musical Theatre)
- 3-year full-time Bachelor of Arts (Arts Management)

Only twenty students per year are accepted into each of the teaching programmes. The three-year full-time theatre training programme is practical in approach and focuses on preparation for careers in the arts and entertainment industry. The curriculum focuses on vocational skills which are underpinned by significant and relevant theoretical studies. In the first year students are not exposed to public performance; in the second and third years WAAPA offers its performers-in-training a comprehensive production repertoire consisting of classical and contemporary theatre, musical theatre, opera, dance (both classical and contemporary) and television.

WAAPA produces and broadcasts a 90 minute telemovie as part of its actor training programme and through corporate sponsorship involves performance students in comprehensive touring programmes throughout Western Australia so that they are prepared for the rigours of regional touring when they enter the profession.

Students are also provided with individual tuition in Alexander technique, vocal studies and, for those who exhibit the necessary skills, in music. Performance students are also taught classical dance, tap, contemporary dance and jazz ballet. All performance students are expected to participate in the Academy choir resulting in fully produced choral and oratorio works.

Training emphasises the students' ability to self-devise theatrical work. Subsequent to their graduation many students have successfully built upon their class-based self-devised activities to generate performance opportunities in the profession, in activities ranging from theatre-in-education to festivals.

Graduates from WAAPA are readily absorbed into the entertainment industry both in Australia and overseas. Presently better than 80% of the graduates work in the industry within twelve months of graduation. More importantly, 70% of those students are still active in the industry ten years after they have graduated.

Students are nurtured during their training and not exposed to industry employers until they have completed their course. Because WAAPA's training is centred in Perth, the institution has a very ambitious and proactive policy of placing its graduates within the entertainment industry. Therefore, final showcase performances take place in Perth, Melbourne and Sydney each year. WAAPA has the lowest attrition rate of any of the three major schools. Students who meet the rigorous demands of the entry requirements are likely to remain within the course to graduation.

WAAPA International

It is hoped that the Western Australian Conservatorium of Music will establish its jazz programmes in New Zealand in 1996 and similar programmes are projected for Indonesia, Malaysia, Thailand and South Korea. The WAAPA's Arts Management programmes are to be franchised into South Africa, Singapore, Malaysia, Thailand and New Zealand, and relationships are being explored with the Royal Academy of Music in London regarding pathways in Musical Theatre and with the Gaiety School of Acting in Dublin to establish joint venture teaching programmes and awards in the performing arts.

WAAPA is proud of its active exchange programme with the London Contemporary Dance School. It has already established a very close relationship with the Amsterdam School of the Arts and will be using that school in future benchmarking exercises along with the Juilliard School in New York and the Australian Institute of Sport in Canberra. Strong links have also been forged with the Slade School of Arts, the University of Humberside and the Surrey Institute of Art and Design.

WAAPA operates a proactive policy in offering training opportunities to Aboriginal Australians, and has successfully placed Aboriginal actors, stage managers and dancers in companies throughout Australia and increasingly students from the Indian Ocean rim with a wide variety of ethnic backgrounds are seeking admission and entering WAAPA courses. International students from India, Malaysia, Singapore, Japan, Sweden, North America and Europe are currently participating in WAAPA courses.

A small selection of degree courses available in Australia offering a substantial practical element.

Australian Academy of Dramatic Arts, PO Box K870, Haymarket, NSW 2000, Tel: 02-318 1544

2- and 3-year Diploma (fee-paying) in Dramatic Arts

University of Western Sydney–Nepean, Faculty of Visual and Performing Arts, PO Box 10, Kingswood NSW 2747, Tel: 047-360 376

3-year Bachelor of Arts (Performance–Acting) or (Theatre, Theory and Practice)
also a BA with Honours and an MA (Performance)

Queensland University of Technology, Kelvin Grove Campus, Locked Bag No. 2, Redhill, Qld 4059, Tel: 07-864 3213

3-year Bachelor of Arts (Drama)

James Cook University of North Queensland, Townsville, Qld 4811, Tel: 077-81 4691

3-year Bachelor of Theatre
4-year (with Honours)

Flinders University of South Australia, Drama Discipline, Bedford Park SA 5042, Tel: 08-201 2637

3-year Bachelor of Arts (Drama)
4-year (with Honours)

Deakin University, Drama and Dance, Rusden Campus, 662 Blackburn Road, Clayton, Victoria 3168, Tel: 03-244 7379

3-year BA Performance Studies
3-year BA Drama

University of Ballarat, PO Box 663, Ballarat, Victoria 3353, Tel: 053-27 9560

3-year BA Performing Arts

University of Tasmania at Launceston, PO Box 1214, Launceston, TAS 7250, Tel: 003-24 3519

3-year BA Theatre
2-year Assoc. Dip. Arts in Drama

Te Kura Toi Whakaari o Aotearoa: New Zealand Drama School

Toi Whakaari: NZ Drama School, PO Box 6690, Wellington, New Zealand, Tel: 04-384 7467

Te Kura Toi Whakaari o Aotearoa: New Zealand Drama School is the government funded National Drama School, centred in the vibrant theatre district of Wellington. It is based on the Michel Saint-Denis concepts of drama schools, with additions and alterations that recognise the New Zealand environment.

The great strengths of Toi Whakaari are:

- Its 25-year tradition of student-centred learning and educational excellence.
- The attentive and nurturing environment of a small intimate school.
- Its flexible inclusion of international tutors and other art forms.
- Its commitment to developing a bicultural school, and the resultant benefits that are provided in performance and in training.
- The reputation it enjoys with more than 250 graduates now informing the range of New Zealand's theatre and film industry.
- The excellent working relationship with all New Zealand theatres, especially the four diverse professional theatres in Wellington.

- A magnificent specialist library with a comprehensive collection of theatre and performance art books, periodicals, audio-visual and archival material.
- An ongoing Open Programme providing workshops for both the profession and community, including an annual two-week workshop festival held in January.

Courses provided:

Diploma of Professional Drama–Acting
Diploma of Professional Theatre–Technical Production
2-year intensive full-time (currently under expansion to 3-year)

Suggestions for Audition Speeches

Male

Shakespeare

Antony and Cleopatra
ENOBARBUS: The barge she sat in, like a burnished throne (II, ii)

Cymbeline
IACHIMO: The crickets sing, and man's o'erlaboured sense (II, ii)

Hamlet
HAMLET: How all occasions do inform against me (IV, iv)

Henry IV, Part One
HOTSPUR: My liege, I did deny no prisoners (I, iii)

Henry V
CHORUS: Now all the youth of England are on fire (II, prologue)
CHORUS: Thus with imagin'd wing our swift scene flies
  (III, prologue)
CHORUS: Now entertain conjecture of a time (IV, prologue)
CHORUS: Vouchsafe to those that have not read the story
  (V, prologue)
BOY: As young as I am, I have observed these three swashers
  (III, ii)

Henry VI, Part Two
YOUNG CLIFFORD: Shame and confusion, all is on the rout!
  (V, ii)

Henry VI, Part Three
GLOUCESTER: What! will the aspiring blood of Lancaster (V, vi)

King John
BASTARD: Mad world! mad kings! mad composition! (II, i)
BASTARD: If thou didst but consent (IV, iii)

King Lear
EDGAR: I heard myself proclaimed (II, iii)

Love's Labour's Lost
DON ARMADO: I do affect the very ground (I, ii)
BEROWNE: And I, – / Forsooth, in love (III, i)
BEROWNE: O, 'tis more than need (IV, iii)

Measure for Measure
ANGELO: What's this? What's this? Is this her fault or mine? (II, ii)

The Merchant of Venice
ARRAGON: And so have I address'd me (II, ix)
BASSANIO: So may the outward shows be least themselves (III, ii)
LAUNCELOT GOBBO: Certainly my conscience will serve me to run (II, ii)
MOROCCO: Some god direct my judgment! (II, vii)
SHYLOCK: Signoir Antonio, many a time and oft (I, iii)

The Merry Wives of Windsor
FALSTAFF: Nay, you shall hear, Master Brook (III, v)
FORD: What a damned Epicurean rascal is this! (II, ii)

A Midsummer Night's Dream
OBERON: My gentle Puck, come hither (II, i)
OBERON: Hast thou the flower there? (II, ii)
PUCK: My mistress with a monster is in love (III, ii)

Much Ado About Nothing
BENEDICK: I do much wonder that one man (II, iii)

Richard II
RICHARD: Needs must I like it well (III, ii)
RICHARD: Discomfortable cousin! know'st thou not (III, ii)
RICHARD: No matter where. Of comfort no man speak (III, ii)
RICHARD: Alack, why am I sent for to a king (IV, i)

Richard III
CLARENCE: O, I have pass'd a miserable night (I, iv)
GLOUCESTER: Was ever woman in this humour woo'd? (I, ii)

The Taming of the Shrew
PETRUCHIO: Thus have I politicly begun my reign (IV, i)

The Tempest
TRINCULO: Here's neither bush nor shrub (II, ii)

Troilus and Cressida
TROILUS: I take to-day a wife and my election (II, ii)
THERSITES: How now, Thersites? (II, iii)

Two Gentlemen of Verona
LAUNCE: Nay, 'twill be this hour ere I have done weeping (II, iii)
LAUNCE: When a man's servant shall play the cur with him (IV, iv)
PROTEUS: To leave my Julia, shall I be foresworn (II, vi)

The Winter's Tale
LEONTES: To your own bents dispose you (I, ii)
TIME: I, that please some, try all, both joy and terror (IV, prologue)

Contemporary

Rodney Ackland: *Absolute Hell*
HUGH (30s): Do you mind if I ask you a question, Miss Monody?

Jean Anouilh: *Thieves' Carnival*
GUSTAVE (20): There, if you think . . .

Aleksei Arbuzov: *The Promise*
LEONIDIK (19): I loved my mother very much . . .

Jim Cartwright: *Road*
SKIN (22): He opens his eyes, he sees you

Anton Chekhov: *The Cherry Orchard*
TROFIMOV (27): Humanity goes forward . . .

Ron Cowen: *Summertree*
YOUNG MAN (20): It's hot out here . . .

Michael Cristofer: *The Shadow Box*
MARK (20s): I mean it's not enough . . .
MARK: When I met Brian . . .

Nikolai Erdman: *The Suicide*
SEMYON (30): What do you think, lad . . .
SEMYON: They don't believe me . . .

Simon Gray: *Butley*
BEN (30): Hate and redemption . . .

Christopher Hampton: *Total Eclipse*
RIMBAUD (19): The first thing he did . . .
VERLAINE (27): Like you, I have one brother . . .

Christopher Hampton: *When Did You Last See My Mother?*
IAN (20): I'm sick of it . . .
JIMMY (20): Once when I was . . .
JIMMY: Well, on Saturday . . .

Barrie Keefe: *Barbarians*
JAN (18): They laughed at me mum . . .

James Kirkwood: *P.S. Your Cat is Dead*
VITO (27): Oh no, men and women . . .

Larry Kramer: *The Normal Heart*
NED (25): I belong to a culture . . .

Eugene O'Neill: *Long Day's Journey into Night*
EDMUND (23): You've just told me . . .
EDMUND: To hell with sense . . .
EDMUND: God, Papa, ever since I went to . . .
EDMUND: For Christ's sake, Papa, forget . . .

Tony Marchant: *The Lucky Ones*
DAVE (20): D'you want to know what life's biggest mystery is?

Tony Marchant: *Welcome Home*
POLO (20): Goldy? Did I tell you . . .

John Osborne: *A Patriot for Me*
REDL (26): Well, I didn't love you . . .
REDL: Oh, stop moaning . . .

Willy Russell: *One For The Road*
DENNIS (28): Everytime I see a new piece of tupperware

Peter Shaffer: *Equus*
ALAN (21): I was pushed forward

Peter Shaffer: *Five Finger Exercise*
WALTER (20): Clive? What's the matter?

Neil Simon: *The Good Doctor*
NARRATOR (*The Drowned Man*): Just getting a little night air . . .
PETER (30s) (*The Seduction*): If I may say so myself . . .

Graham Swannell: *Stuttgart (State of Affairs)*
TERENCE (30): No, these days, I can't get away from my first thought . . .

Frank Wedekind: *Spring Awakening*
HANS (16): Have you prayed tonight, Desdemona?

MORITZ (16): Just a word, that's all it needed . . .
MORITZ: I refuse to cry again today . . .

Michael Weller: *Loose Ends*
PAUL (20s): It was great at the beginning . . .

Arnold Wesker: *Chips with Everything*
PIP (18): One day when I was . . .
PIP: The started to build . . .
SMILER (18): Leave me alone . . .

Nigel Williams: *Class Enemy*
RACKS (16): My ol' man . . .
SNATCH (16): I started on winders

Female

Shakespeare

All's Well That Ends Well
HELENA: O! were that all. I think not on my father (I, i)
HELENA: 'Till I have no wife, I have nothing in France.' (III, ii)

As You Like It
ROSALIND: It is not the fashion to see the lady the epilogue
(Epilogue)

Cymbeline
IMOGEN: I see a man's life is a tedious one (III, vi)
IMOGEN: Yes, sir, to Milford-Haven (IV, ii)

Henry VI, Part Three
QUEEN MARGARET: Brave warriors, Clifford and Northumberland
(I, iv)
QUEEN MARGARET: Great Lords – wise men ne'er sit and wail their
loss (V, iv)

Henry VIII
KATHARINE: Sir, I desire you do me right and justice (II, iv)

Julius Caesar
PORTIA: You've ungently, Brutus (II, i)

King John
CONSTANCE: Gone to be married! gone to swear a peace! (III, i)
CONSTANCE: A wicked day, and not a holy day! (III, i)

Love's Labour's Lost
PRINCESS: A time, methinks, too short (V, ii)

The Merchant of Venice
PORTIA: I pray you, tarry: pause a day or two (III, ii)
PORTIA: You see me, Lord Bassanio, where I stand (III, ii)

Merry Wives of Windsor
MISTRESS PAGE: What! Have I scaped love letters . . . (II, i)

A Midsummer Night's Dream
HELENA: How happy some o'er other some can be! (I, i)
HELENA: Lo! she is one of this confederacy (III, ii)
TITANIA: These are the forgeries of jealousy (II, i)

Othello
EMILIA: Yes, and a dozen, and as many . . . (IV, iii)

Richard III
LADY ANNE: Set down, set down your honourable load (I, ii)
LADY ANNE: What! do you tremble? Are you all afraid? (I, ii)

Troilus and Cressida
CRESSIDA: By the same token, you are a bawd (I, ii)
CRESSIDA: Hard to seem won; but I was won, my lord (III, ii)

Two Gentlemen of Verona
JULIA: This barble shall not hence forth trouble me (I, ii)
JULIA: A virtuous gentlewoman, mild and beautiful (IV, iv)

The Winter's Tale
HERMIONE: Since what I am to say must be but that (III, ii)
HERMIONE: Sir, spare your threats (III, ii)
PAULINA: What studied torments, tyrant, hast for me? (III, ii)

Contemporary

Jay Allen: *The Prime of Miss Jean Brodie*
MISS BRODIE (35): Little girls, I am in the business . . .

Maxwell Anderson: *Winterset*
MIRIAMNE (15): Mio, I'd have gone . . .

B. Brecht: *Fear and Misery in The Third Reich*
JEWISH WIFE (40s): Yes, I'm packing . . .

Caryl Churchill: *Cloud Nine*
BETTY (20s): I used to think Clive was the one . . .

Michael Cristofer: *The Shadow Box*
AGNES (30s): We were very close . . .

Andrew Davies: *Rose*
SALLY (30s): Saw one today, on me way home from the library . . .

John Van Druten: *I am a Camera*
SALLY (20s): Well, there is a man . . .

Michael Frayn: *Donkeys' Years*
LADY DRIVER (35): Brown Corduroy trousers . . .

Jean Genet: *The Balcony*
CARMEN (20s): Excuse me . . .

William Hanley: *Slow Dance on the Killing Ground*
ROSIE (19): If you knew me better . . .

David Hare: *Plenty*
SUSAN (25): Mr Medlicott has moved into my office.

Fay and Michael Kanin: *Rashomon*
WIFE (30s): He's gone . . he's gone . . .

Arthur Kopit: *Chamber Music*
WOMAN IN A SAFARI SUIT (30s): You see, I've spent . . .

Mary Martin: *Gertrude Stein*
GERTRUDE – any section of monologue

David Mercer: *After Haggerty*
CLAIRE (20s): James Mawnen Haggerty, I'm going . . .
CLAIRE: Don't say it, Haggerty . . .

Anthony Minghella: *Made in Bangkok*
FRANCES (28): No, not because of Stephen . . .

Peter Nichols: *A Day in the Death of Joe Egg*
SHEILA (35): One of these days . . .

Eugene O'Neill: *Anna Christie*
ANNA (20): I suppose if I tried to tell you . . .

Eugene O'Neill: *A Touch of the Poet*
SARAH (20): Oh, Mother, it's a great joke on me . . .

Alexander Ostrovsky: *The Storm*
KATHERINE (20): I used to be so . . .

Jean-Paul Sartre: *Huis Clos (In Camera)*
ESTELLE (30s): All right, which one of you . . .

George Bernard Shaw: *Mrs Warren's Profession*
VIVIE (20s): Mother, you don't know at all . . .

George Bernard Shaw: *Widowers' Houses*
BLANCHE (20s): Well? So you have come back here . . .

Neil Simon: *The Good Doctor*
WIFE (30s) *(The Seduction)*: No, no, not a word . . .

Tom Stoppard: *Jumpers*
DOTTY (20s): And yet, professor . . .
DOTTY: Well, it's all over . . .

Peter Weiss: *The Marat/Sade*
CORDAY (24): In my room in Caen . . .

Tennessee Williams: *Cat on a Hot Tin Roof*
MAGGIE (30): I know, believe me . . .

Tennessee Williams: *Talk to Me Like the Rain and Let Me Listen*
WOMAN (30s): I will receive a cheque . . .

Victoria Wood: *Up To You, Porky*
GUIDE (22): Right, I'm your official guide . . .

The National Council for Drama Training

The National Council for Drama Training (NCDT) was established in 1976, following the report of the committee of inquiry set
up by the Calouste Gulbenkian Foundation into professional
training for drama, which was published in 1975 under the title
Going on the Stage.

The NCDT is an independent body, registered as a charity and
financed by its member organisations – the British Actors' Equity
Association, the British Broadcasting Corporation, Theatrical
Management Association, the Society of West End Theatres, the
Conference of Drama Schools, Channel Four Television and
donations from a number of the independent television companies. The Council itself consists of eighteen representatives –
six each from the union, the employers' organisations and the
drama schools – plus an independent chairman. Meetings of the
Council are also attended by observers from other organisations
with an interest in professional training for drama, such as the
Department of Education and Science, the Local Education
Authority Associations, the Council for National Academic
Awards, the Standing Committee of University Drama Depart-
ments, the Drama and Theatre Education Council, the Arts
Council and the Association of British Theatre Technicians.

The NCDT exists in order to encourage the highest possible
standards of vocational education and training, and to provide a
forum within which the different sides of the profession can
discuss matters of common interest in relation to training. The
Council is particularly concerned to promote the closest possible
links between those engaged in training and those working in the
profession. From the outset the Council attached importance to
maintaining only a minimum of central organisation. It is therefore run on a very limited budget by a part-time secretariat, to
whom any inquiries should be directed.

Since its establishment in 1976, the NCDT has always seen, and continues to see, the accreditation of courses as its first priority. There are four reasons for this: the contribution accreditation makes in helping to raise the standard of drama training generally; the guidance that an NCDT list of accredited courses gives to local education authorities as they reach decisions on student grants, which are mainly available only for vocational education and training for drama on a discretionary basis; the promotion of closer links between the profession and the training sector; and the hope that accreditation will help to make entry into the profession a smoother process for those graduating from accredited courses.

The accreditation process was announced by the NCDT in October 1978. It was a two-stage process whereby schools had first to satisfy the NCDT that they met certain qualifying criteria before a visit to consider their courses took place. An accreditation board of eminent people from all sides of the profession was assembled, from among whom the visiting panels for each course were made up.

The accreditation boards are now in the process of visiting, to consider for re-accreditation, those courses for which the accreditation period is about to expire.

Drama schools with courses at present accredited by the NCDT are set out below.

Two- and Three-year Courses

Academy of Live and Recorded Arts
The Arts Educational London Schools
Birmingham School of Speech and Drama
Bristol Old Vic Theatre School
Rose Bruford College of Speech and Drama
The Central School of Speech and Drama
Cygnet Training Theatre
Drama Centre London
East 15 Acting School
Guildford School of Acting
Guildhall School of Music and Drama
London Academy of Music and Dramatic Art
Manchester Metropolitan University
Mountview Theatre School
Queen Margaret College
Royal Academy of Dramatic Art
Royal Scottish Academy of Music and Drama

Webber-Douglas Academy of Dramatic Art
Welsh College of Music and Drama

One-year Postgraduate Courses

Drama Studio London
Guildford School of Acting
Mountview Theatre School
Webber-Douglas Academy of Dramatic Art
Welsh College of Music and Drama

Stage Management Courses

Bristol Old Vic Theatre School
Rose Bruford College of Speech and Drama
Central School of Speech and Drama
Guildford School of Acting
Guildhall School of Music and Drama
London Academy of Music and Dramatic Art
Mountview Theatre School
Royal Academy of Dramatic Art
Rose Bruford Collge of Speech and Drama
Royal Scottish Academy of Music and Drama
Welsh College of Music and Drama

Careers Information and Grant-making Bodies

Some of these books and pamphlets may be available at public libraries.

Careers information sheets
Careers with Music
Museums and Art Galleries
Opportunities in Leisure and Recreation
Radio, TV, Theatre, Cinema

Central Services Unit for University Careers and Appointment Services, Crawford House, Precinct Centre, Oxford Road, Manchester M13 9E, Tel: 0161-273 4233

Grants to Students: A Brief Guide
Department for Education, Sanctuary Buildings, Great Smith Street, London SW1P 3BT, Tel: 0171-925 5000

The Grants Register
Macmillan Press, 4 Little Essex Street, London WC2R 3LF, Tel: 0171-836 6633

Sponsorship and Supplementary Awards
Careers and Occupational Information Centre (COIC), PO Box 348, Bristol BS99 7FE, Tel: 0114-259 4569

Directory of Grant-making Trusts
Charities Aid Foundation, 48 Pembury Road, Tonbridge, Kent TN9 2JD, Tel: 01732-771333

The Charities Digest
Family Welfare Association, 6 Butterworths, 501 Kingsland Road, London E8 4AU, Tel: 0181-742 9209

Studying Abroad/Work Experience Abroad
The British Council, Medlock Street, Manchester M15 4AA,
Tel: 0161-957 7000

Study Abroad (UNESCO International Handbook)
UNESCO, 7 Place de Fontenoy, 75700 Paris, France
(also available from HMSO)

Scholarship Guide for Commonwealth Postgraduate Students
Association of Commonwealth Universities, 36 Gordon Square,
London WC1 0PF, Tel: 0171-387 8572

Further information available from:
Educational Grants Advisory Service, 501–505 Kingsland Road,
Dalston, London E8 4AU, Tel: 0171-923 3513

Useful Organisations

The Actors' Centres

South:
1A Tower Street, London WC2H 9NP, Tel: 0171-240 3940

North:
The Old School, Little John Street, Manchester M3 4PQ,
Tel: 0161-832 3430

Essentially these are professional bases for everyone in the entertainment industry and will be places you will want to use once you have trained and are an Equity member. Many Equity members have never had the chance of a full-time training, either because they've been too busy or because of financial restrictions. The Actors' Centres offer opportunities to actors supporting themselves, with part-time work between acting jobs, to follow a series of very useful classes over a period of time, meeting and working with fellow professionals in a non-competitive atmosphere, and experiencing some of the more specialist areas covered by a full-time training course. The tutors are of a high standard and the classes include acting, audition text, verse speaking, dialect, voice, singing, television, radio, fencing, movement, dance, tap, keep-fit, musicals, yoga and T'ai Chi. Other amenities include a green room and servery for light meals. In each schedule of events are included special projects, including talks and meetings with visiting directors, designers and writers, plus TV workshops and short courses. Observers are admitted to some classes and events.

Association of British Theatre Technicians

47 Bermondsey Street, London SE1 3XT, Tel: 0171-403 3778

This association was formed in 1961. It collects and disseminates information in all relevant fields to its members and to bodies who consult it. This is done by specialist committees dealing at present with theatre planning, training, safety, lighting, sound, materials and management, each of which provides expert advice for interested bodies and individuals and produces information sheets and data sheets for circulation to members.

The ABTT is recognised as an authoritative body and liaises with such organisations as the Arts Council, the Home Office and the Department of the Environment. It gives technical advice to the Theatre Advisory Council.

The standard work *Theatre Planning* is now in its second edition and there are five codes of practice booklets in print for safe working with more in the pipeline.

British Actors' Equity (including Variety Artists' Federation)

Guild House, Upper St Martin's Lane, London WC2H 9EG, Tel: 0171-379 6000

The union for actors, directors, designers, choreographers and variety artists.

British Film Institute

National Film Archive, 21 Stephen Street, London W1P 1PL, Tel: 0171-255 1444

Broadcasting and Entertainment Trades Alliance (BETA)

111 Wardour Street, London W1V 4AY, Tel: 0171-437 8506

The union that covers most of the technical trades.

National Council for Drama Training

5 Tavistock Place, London WC1H 9SS, Tel: 0171-387 3650

National Drama Festival Association (NDFA)

Mrs Brenda Nicholl, 24 Jubilee Road, Formby, Liverpool L37 2HT, Tel: 017048-72421

National Operatic and Dramatic Association (NODA)

1 Crestfield Street, London WC1H 8AU, Tel: 0171-837 5655

NODA supports and promotes the production of amateur musicals, operettas and revues around the country and serves as a hire department for scripts, scores and librettos. From time to time it publishes a newsletter for members and organises short drama, movement or singing courses all over the UK to improve the standard of amateur performance.

National Student Drama Festival

20 Lansdowne Road, London N10 2AU, Tel: 0181-883 4586

Sponsored by *The Sunday Times*, among others, and now in its fortieth year, this is the only regular focus for British student drama. This unique travelling marathon changes venue each year and presents plays, workshops and discussions, plus several social events. After a process of selection by travelling adjudicators, twenty pieces are brought together for an eight-day event, usually in April.

Research Training Initiatives

18–20 Dean Street, Newcastle upon Tyne NE1 1PG, Tel: 0191-261 6581

Shape

1 Thorpe Close, London W10 5XL, Tel: 0181-960 9245

Shape is an arts organisation, established in 1976, which creates opportunities for people with any kind of disability or mental illness, the ill, elderly or severely socially disadvantaged to participate in arts activities and events. Much of the work takes the form of initiating regular weekly arts workshops in hospitals, day centres, homes, hostels and other institutions. Increasingly, Shape is involved in organising similar activities in the open community using local arts and community venues. Shape also runs a ticket scheme, which distributes reduced-price tickets to London's arts venues, offers a free booking service and organises volunteer driver/escorts; tours professional companies and groups; tours exhibitions of contemporary prints and photographs with programmes of related practical activities; offers training courses for artists and staff of institutions; works with arts and community centres to increase their provision for people with disabilities and special needs; and works with other arts and voluntary bodies to establish initiatives such as Artsline, the Access and Information Group, Arts Access, Fair Play: the Campaign for Equal Opportunities in the Arts for People with Disabilities, and No Kidding.

Speech and Drama Magazine

14 Florence Road, Brighton, East Sussex BN1 6DJ

The Spotlight

7 Leicester Place, London WC2H 7BP, Tel: 0171-437 7631

Theatrical Management Association (TMA)

Bedford Chambers, The Piazza, Covent Garden, London WC2E 8HQ, Tel: 0171-836 0971

Founded in 1894 by Sir Henry Irving, the TMA now represents over 400 British theatres and companies except those of the West End of London and the London fringe. Its members include subsidised managements, local authorities, theatre owners, commercial producers and managers, opera and ballet companies, children's theatre and community theatre. Its involvement in theatre is wide and covers training seminars and representation on a variety of other bodies as well as being responsible for negotiating national agreements with the theatre unions.

APPENDIX V

Young People's Theatre Companies

A selection of companies where opportunities exist to participate in workshops and productions are listed below.

Yvonne Arnaud Theatre, Millbrook, Guildford, Surrey GU1 3UX

Barnstormers' Youth Theatre, 107 Ladies Mile Road, Patcham, Brighton, East Sussex

Basildon Youth Theatre Scheme, c/o Towngate Theatre, Towngate, Basildon, Essex SS14 1DW

Bishop's Stortford Youth Theatre, SNAP People's Theatre Trust, Millats One House, Southmill Road, Bishop's Stortford, Herts. CM23 3DH

Contact Theatre Community Drama Team, The Brickhouse, Devas Street, Manchester M15 6JA

Croydon Young People's Theatre, Ashcroft Theatre, Fairfield Halls, Park Lane, Croydon CR9 1OG

Gorton Workshop, 18 Hawthorn Grove, Heaton Moor, Stockport, Cheshire

Greenwich Young People's Theatre, Burrage Road, London SE18 7JZ

Langley Theatre Group, Adult Education Centre, Wood Street, Middleton, Manchester M24 3TS

London Irish Youth Theatre, Victor House, Marlborough Gardens, Whetstone, London N20 0SH

Manchester Youth Theatre, 57 Hulme Hall Road, Cheadle Hume, Stockport SK18 6JX

Merseyside Young People's Theatre Company, 5 Hope Street, Liverpool L1 9BH

National Association of Youth Theatres, Unit 1304 The Custard Factory, Gibb St Digbeth, Birmingham B9 4AA

National Youth Music Theatre, Sadlers Wells Theatre, Rosebery Avenue, London EC1R 4TN

National Youth Theatre, Shaw Theatre, 443–445 Holloway Road, London N7 6LW

Royal Court Young People's Theatre, 309 Portobello Road, London W10 5TD

Solihull Youth Theatre, The Drama Centre, Silvermere Road, Sheldon, Birmingham

Young National Trust Theatre, National Trust, 36 Queen Anne's Gate, London SW1H 9AS

Young Vic, The Cut, London SE1 8LP

Arts Councils and Regional Arts Boards

Arts Councils

England
14 Great Peter Street, London SW1P 3NQ, Tel: 0171-333 0100

Scotland
12 Manor Place, Edinburgh EH3 7DD, Tel: 0131-226 6051

Wales
Holst House, 9 Museum Place, Cardiff CF1 3NX,
Tel: 01222-394711

Northern Ireland
185 Stranmillis Road, Belfast BT9 5DU, Tel: 01232-381591

Regional Arts Boards

East Midlands Arts
Mountfields House, Epinal Way, Loughborough, Leicestershire
LE11 0QE, Tel: 01509-218292

Eastern Arts
Cherry Hinton Hall, Cherry Hinton Road, Cambridge CB1 4DW,
Tel: 01223-215355

London Arts Board
133 Long Acre, London WC2E 9AF, Tel: 0171-240 1313

North West Arts
12 Harter Street, Manchester M1 6HY, Tel: 0161-228 3062

Northern Arts
10 Osborne Terrace, Newcastle upon Tyne NE2 1NZ, Tel: 0191-281 6334

South East Arts
10 Mount Ephraim, Tunbridge Wells, Kent TN4 8AS, Tel:
01892-515210

South West Arts
Bradninch Place, Gandy Street, Exeter, Devon EX4 3LS,
Tel: 01392-218188

Southern Arts
13 Clement Street, Winchester, Hants SO23 9DQ, Tel:
01962-855099

West Midlands Arts
82 Granville Street, Birmingham B1 2LH, Tel: 0121-631 3121

Yorkshire and Humberside Arts
21 Bond Street, Dewsbury, West Yorkshire WF13 1AX,
Tel: 01924-455555

Further Reading

Professional Guides

Barkworth Peter, *About Acting* (London, Secker & Warburg, 1980)

Griffiths, Trevor R., *Stagecraft* (Oxford, Phaidon Press, 1990)

Hayman, Ronald, *The Set-up* (London, Eyre Methuen, 1974)

Smalley, Ken, *So You Want to Work in the Theatre* (for technicians) (London, Association of British Theatre Technicians handbook)

Swift, Clive, *The Job of Acting* (London, Harrap, 1984)

Theatre History

Esslin, Martin, *The Anatomy of Drama* (London, Sphere Books, 1978)

Esslin, Martin, *The Theatre of the Absurd* (Harmondsworth, Penguin, 1987)

Granville-Barker, Harley, *Prefaces to Shakespeare* (London, Batsford, 1982–5)

Hartnoll, Phyllis, *Oxford Companion to the Theatre* (Oxford, Oxford University Press, 1983)

Hobson, Harold, *Theatre in Britain* (Oxford, Phaidon Press, 1984)

Nicoll, Allardyce, *British Drama* (London, Harrap, 1978)

Nicoll, Allardyce, *The English Theatre* (London, Harrap, 1936)

Nicoll, Allardyce, *Readings in British Drama* (London, Harrap, 1928)

Styan, J. L., *Shakespeare's Stagecraft* (Cambridge, Cambridge University Press, 1967)

Wickham, Glynne, *A History of the Theatre* (Oxford, Phaidon Press, 1985)

Williams, Raymond, *Drama from Ibsen to Brecht* (Harmondsworth, Penguin, 1973)

Acting and Improvisation

Barker, Clive, *Theatre Games* (London, Methuen, 1977)

Barton, John, *Playing Shakespeare* (London, Methuen, 1984)

Benedetti, Robert, *The Actor at Work* (Englewood Cliffs, New Jersey, Prentice-Hall, 1994)

Hagen, Uta, *Respect for Acting* (London, Macmillan, 1973)

Hagen, Uta, *A Challenge for the Actor* (New York, Scribners, 1991)

Johnstone, Keith, *Impro: Improvisation and the Theatre* (London, Methuen, 1981)

Marowitz, Charles, *The Act of Being* (London, Secker & Warburg, 1978)

Redgrave, Michael, *The Actor's Ways and Means* (London, Heinemann Education, 1979)

Saint-Denis, Michel, *Training for the Theatre* (London, Heinemann, 1982)

Seyler, Athene, and Stephen Haggard, *The Craft of Comedy* (New York, Theatre Arts, 1957)

Spolin, Viola, *Improvisation for the Theatre*, rev. ed. (Evanston, Ill., North Western University Press, 1983)

Stanislavsky, Konstantin, *An Actor Prepares*, rev. ed. (London, Methuen, 1980)

Stanislavsky, Konstantin, *Building a Character*, rev. ed. (London, Methuen, 1979)

Stanislavsky, Konstantin, *My Life in Art*, rev. ed. (London, Methuen, 1980)

Alexander Technique

Alexander, F. M., *The Use of Self* (London, Gollancz, 1985)

Barlow, Wilfrid, *The Alexander Principle* (London, Arrow Books, 1975)

Hodgkinson, Liz, *Alexander Technique* (London, Piatkus Books, 1988)

Voice

Berry, Cicely, *The Actor and his Text* (London, Virgin, 1993)

Berry, Cicely, *Voice and the Actor* (London, Virgin, 1993)

Colson, Greta, *Voice Production and Speech* (London, Pitman Publishing, 1988)

Linklater, Kristin, *Freeing Shakespeare's Voice* (TCG, New York, 1992)
Linklater, Kristin, *Freeing the Natural Voice* (TCG, New York, 1976)
McCallion, Michael, *The Voice Book* (London, Faber, 1989)
Rodenburg, Patsy, *The Need ford Words* (London, Methuen, 1992)
Rodenburg, Patsy, *The Right to Speak* (London, Methuen, 1993)
Turner, Clifford (ed.), *Voice and Speech in the Theatre* (London, A & C Black, 1993)

Periodicals

Amateur Stage (0171-486 1732)
Arts Centres UK Quarterly (01325-465930)
London Theatre Guide
London Theatre Record (0181-892 6087)
London Theatre Visitor
New Theatre Quarterly (01223-333333)
Plays International (0171-720 1950)
Plays and Players (0171-343 8515)
Shape News (0181-960 9245)
Sightline
The Stage (incorporating Television Today) (0171-403 1818)
Theatre Review
Time Out (0171-813 3000)
Variety (USA) (0171-637 3663)
The Visitor
What's On (0171-278 4393)

Australia and New Zealand

Carey, Dean, *The Actors Audition Manual* (Currency Press, Sydney, Australia, 1985)
Carey, Dean, *Masterclass, The Actors Audition Manual Volume II – Male and Female Editions* (Currency Press, Sydney, Australia, 1995)

Index